MW01199171

Angora Rabbits

The moral rights of the author has been asserted

British Library Cataloguing in Publication Data

A catalogue record for this book is available from the British Library

ISBN 978-1-909820-07-4

Disclaimer and Legal Notice

While every attempt has been made to verify the information shared in this publication, neither shall the author nor publisher assume any responsibility for errors, omissions, nor contrary interpretation of the subject matter herein. Any perceived slight to any specific person(s) or organisation(s) are purely unintentional. You need to do your own due diligence to determine if the content of this product is correct for you.

This book is presented solely for educational and entertainment purposes. The author and publisher are not offering it as legal, accounting, or other professional services advice. While best efforts have been used in preparing this book, the author, affiliates and publisher make no representations or warranties of any kind and assume no liabilities of any kind with respect to the accuracy or completeness of the contents and specifically disclaim any implied warranties of merchantability or fitness of use for a particular purpose. Neither shall the author nor the publisher be held liable or responsible to any person or entity with respect to any loss or incidental or consequential damages caused, or alleged to have been caused, directly or indirectly, by the information or programs contained herein. The author shall not be liable for any loss incurred as a consequence of the use and application, direct or indirectly, of any information presented in this work. This publication is designed to provide information in regard to the subject matter covered. It is the reader's responsibility to find advice before putting anything written in the book into practice.

References are provided for informational purposes only and do not constitute endorsement of any websites or other sources. Readers should be aware that the websites listed in this book may change. We have no control over the nature, content, and availability of the websites listed in this book. The inclusion of any website links does not necessarily imply a recommendation or endorse the views expressed within them. EKL Publishing takes no responsibility for, and will not be liable for, the website being temporally unavailable or being removed from the internet. The information in this book is not intended to serve as legal advice.

Angora Rabbits

The Pet Owner's Guide

Includes English, French, Giant, Satin and German Breeds.
Buying, Care, Lifespan, Colors, Diet, Health,
Breeders, Facts, are all covered

Ann L. Fletcher

Foreword

Hello and thank you for buying my book.

I hope that this book will provide a straightforward and practical guide to help you prepare for and look after your Angora Rabbit. I've included in this book information about their care, habitat, cost, diet, cages, facts, set up, breeds, life span, feeding, health, breeding and a care sheet. After reading this book you will be a lot more confident in looking after your Angora Rabbit!

I have written this book using American spelling as that is what I'm used to. I have given measurements in both feet and inches/pounds and ounces and also in metric. I have also given costs in US$ and GBP. Both the measurements and costs are approximate guides. I have done my best to ensure the accuracy of the information in this book as at the time of publication. I've kept the style deliberately simple so as children will find it easy to read.

I trust that after reading this book you will enjoy the experience of owning and looking after an Angora Rabbit and that you will have a wonderful time enjoying the pleasure they bring in the years to come!

All good wishes, Ann L. Fletcher

Acknowledgements

I never would have been able to complete this book without the care and support of my family. My husband John has been the silent partner in helping me put together all my little books on rabbits. He has always been there for me through every endeavor, the good times and the maddening and I thank him for his love and support.

Thanks also to my children Mark and Stacey for their continuing enthusiasm for my latest project and helping me out around the house when things got out of control. Special thanks to my dear friend Katherine who came up trumps with her experiences and stories of her Angora Rabbits which was a great help.

Table of Contents

Chapter One: Introduction *1*

Useful Terms to Know 2

Chapter Two: Understanding Them *4*

1.) What Are Angora Rabbits?...5

2.) Facts About Angora Rabbits 6

Summary of Facts...8

3.) History of Angora Rabbits as Pets 9

a.) History of the ARBA.. 10

b.) History of the BRC 11

c.) Angora Rabbit Breed Clubs 11

4.) Types of Angora Rabbits 15

5.) Colors of Angora Rabbits 18

Chapter Three: What to Know Before You Buy *23*

1.) Do You Need a License?...24

a.) Licensing in the U.S.A. 24

b.) Licensing in the U.K. 25

c.) Licensing Elsewhere.. 25

2.) How Many Should You Buy? 26

3.) Can Angora Rabbits Be Kept with Other Pets? 27

4.) Ease and Cost of Care 28

a.) Initial Costs 29

b.) Monthly Costs 32

c.) Time Considerations 34

5.) Pros and Cons of Angora Rabbits 35

6.) Human Health Considerations 37

Chapter Four: Purchasing Angora Rabbits *38*

1.) **Where to Buy Angora Rabbits** **39**
   a.) Buying in the U.S.A. 39
   b.) Buying in the U.K. 41

2.) **How to Select a Healthy Angora Rabbit** **43**

Chapter Five: Caring for Angora Rabbits **46**

1.) **Habitat Requirements** **47**
   a.) General Habitat Requirements 47
   b.) Benefits of Different Cage Types...................... 49
   c.) Keeping Angoras Indoors vs. Outdoors 51
   d.) Recommended Cage Accessories.................... 52

2.) **Feeding Angora Rabbits** **55**
   a.) Basic Nutritional Needs 55
   b.) Commercial Rabbit Pellets 58
   c.) Supplemental Food and Treats...................... 59
   d.) General Feeding Tips for Rabbits: 60

3.) **Litter Training Your Rabbit** **61**
   a.) Steps to Litter Training 61

4.) **Tips for Grooming Angoras** **62**
   a.) Step-by-Step Grooming Guide 64
   b.) Steps for Hand-Plucking 66
   c.) Steps for Shearing Wool 66
   d.) Spinning Angora Wool 68

Chapter Six: Breeding Angora Rabbits..................... **71**

1.) **Basic Breeding Information**................................**72**

2.) **The Breeding Process**..**73**

3.) **Raising the Babies** **75**

Chapter Seven: Keeping Healthy **79**

1.) **Common Health Problems** **81**
   Colibacillosis 81
   Dental Problems 81
   Dermatophytosis 82
   Enterotoxemia... 83
   Fleas/Mites.. 83

Listeriosis.. 84

Mastitis... 85

Myxomatosis 85

Otitis Media 86

Papillomatosis 87

Parasites 87

Pasteurella.. 88

Pneumonia 89

Rhinitis.. 89

Uterine Cancer 90

Viral Hemorrhagic Disease 90

Wool Block 91

2.) Preventing Illness 92

a.) Recommended Vaccinations 93

b.) Dangerous/Toxic Foods....................................... 94

c.) Ears, Eyes, Nails and Teeth 94

3.) Pet Insurance 97

Chapter Eight: Showing Angora Rabbits...................101

1.) Breed Standard 102

a.) UK Angora Breed Standard.................................. 102

b.) ARBA English Angora Breed Standard 104

2.) What to Know Before Showing 107

3.) Things to Bring to a Rabbit Show........................109

Chapter Nine: Angora Rabbit Care Sheet.................110

1.) Basic Information 111

2.) Cage Set-up Guide 112

3.) Nutrition and Feeding Facts 112

4.) Breeding and Rearing Facts................................113

5.) Planning for the Unexpected 114

Chapter Ten: General Care Questions.....................117

Chapter Eleven: Relevant Websites.........................122

Shopping 122

1.) Food for Angora Rabbits 124

2.) Care for Angora Rabbits 125

3.) Health Information for Angora Rabbits 126

4.) General Information for Angora Rabbits............. 127

5.) Showing Angora Rabbits 128

Index.. 130

Photo Credits 136

References 144

Chapter One: Introduction

Take a moment to imagine a giant ball of soft white fur with a pink nose and two ears sticking up out of it. This image is not far from the reality of the Angora Rabbit. These rabbits have traditionally been bred for their long, thick fur that can be spun into wool. They have also been proven to make a most wonderful and popular pet. You will have a hard time finding another breed of rabbit as friendly and active as Angoras!

In this book, you have a superb resource giving the information that you need to prepare and care for your Angora Rabbit.

Starting with basic facts about this delightful breed and ending with valuable reference sites, this book provides a wonderful guide to help you become a responsible owner. These rabbits make wonderful pets, bonding closely with their human companions and often getting along with other household pets.

If you want to ensure that your rabbit receives the best care possible, I hope you will find the facts I've provided helpful and informative. I trust that in reading my book, you will find the answers to your questions. I have included material I believe to be appropriate in assisting you in selecting and purchasing your rabbit as well as tips for housing, feeding and breeding your pet. By the time you finish this book I know you will feel a lot more confident and ready to provide excellent care for your Angora Rabbit!

Useful Terms to Know

- **Buck**: a male rabbit
- **Cross Breeding**: breeding two different breeds together
- **Crown**: refers to a prominent ridge and crest along the top of the head extending to the base of the ears
- **Dam**: the mother of a rabbit
- **Doe**: a female rabbit
- **Hock**: the joint of the rabbit's foot
- **Inbreeding**: breeding two closely related rabbits to each other (e.g. brother to sister)

- **Junior**: young rabbit between 14 weeks and 5 months

- **Kindling**: process of giving birth to a litter of kits

- **Kit**: a baby rabbit

- **Litter**: two or more baby rabbits resulting from a single pregnancy/kindling

- **Lopped**: pendulous ears (opposite of erect ears)

- **Stud Buck**: a male rabbit suitable for breeding

- **Sire**: the father of a rabbit

- **Weaning**: the process through which kits begin to eat more solid food and rely less on nursing

Chapter Two: Understanding Them

A s you will learn in reading this book, Angora Rabbits are a superb breed to keep as pets but have also been and continue to be farmed commercially in different parts of the world.

These rabbits produce thick wool that can be spun and used for knitting yarn and in the production of clothing such as sweaters and suits as well as in the manufacture of felt. As Angora Rabbits have such unique uses, they are a very popular breed. Before you go out and buy one however, you should take the time to learn the basics about them. In this chapter you will learn key facts about the Angora Rabbit including the different breeds and their history as pets.

1.) What Are Angora Rabbits?

Angora Rabbits are a breed of domestic rabbit known for their long, soft wool. These rabbits are one of the oldest domesticated breeds, having originated in Ankara, Turkey. This breed has a long history of popularity as pets as well as commercial use in raising wool for spinning yarn. They first appeared in the U.S.A. in the early 20th century and have since become incredibly popular in the pet industry.

There are four different breeds of Angora Rabbit: English, French, Giant and Satin. A fifth breed the German Angora, is not accepted by the American Rabbit Breeders' Association (ARBA) but remains popular in the United States of America.

Angora wool is both finer and softer than cashmere while recognized for its silky texture which grows at a rate of about 1 inch (2.54 cm) per month. This softness makes it much warmer and lighter than wool due to the hollow core of its thin fibers and is referred to by knitters as a halo but what we would commonly refer to as fluffiness. Because their coats are so long and plush, these rabbits often have the appearance of being a round, white snowball. Depending on the breed, even the face of the rabbit may be entirely covered with hair.

One of the main benefits of keeping Angora Rabbits as pets is that their wool doesn't have the same allergy-causing qualities that many other pets have. Additionally, Angoras are very social and playful – they can form close bonds with their owners and often enjoy the company of other rabbits and household pets. If you are thinking about keeping a rabbit as a family pet, or even raising one for wool, the Angora Rabbit is an excellent choice to consider.

2.) Facts About Angora Rabbits

Though the details may vary by breed, Angora Rabbits are typically short and compact in body with a full chest and rounded shoulders. The head is short and broad, set close to the body and well up from the ground. The ears themselves should be short and fringed, carried in a V close to the head. According to the breed standard, the eyes should be bold and bright, the legs medium-fine boned and covered with good quality wool.

In terms of showing Angoras, one of the key considerations about wool is the density of it. The ideal length is between

3.5 to 7 inches (8.89 to 17.8 cm), though it can certainly grow longer. Angora Rabbits come in a variety of sizes but are generally divided into two classifications – white and colored. All colored Angoras exhibit some degree of banding in their coats because their coats are made up of many layers which darken slightly as they extend toward the tip of the fur.

As I've mentioned, the appearance and size of Angoras varies slightly according to the specific breed. Below you will find the size information and a few key facts to differentiate the various breeds:

English Angora: English Angoras typically weigh about 4.5 to 8 lbs. (2.04 to 3.63 kg) and they are known for their puppy-like facial features.

French Angora: The French Angora is slightly larger than the English Angora, weighing between 7.5 and 10 lbs. (3.4 to 4.54 kg) at maturity.

Giant Angora: The Giant Angora breed reaches a weight of 12 lbs. (5.44 kg) or more at maturity. Its coat contains three types of wool – a soft under wool, awn fluff and awn hair.

Satin Angora: The Satin Angora is about the same size as the French Angora, weighing between 7 and 10 lbs. (3.18 to 4.54 kg) at maturity.

German Angora: The average size of a German Angora rabbit ranges from about 4.5 to 12 lbs. (2.04 to 5.44 kg).

In addition to their soft, wooly coats, Angora Rabbits are also known for their friendly personalities. These rabbits tend to get along with everyone – they can even get along with well-mannered dogs and cats! If properly cared for and given adequate attention, Angora Rabbits can form close bonds with their owners and will even develop individual personalities. Angoras can be very playful and enjoy having plastic balls, pieces of wood and chew toysto play with.

Summary of Facts

Classification: wool breed

Weight: varies by breed 4.5 to 12 lbs. plus (2.04 to 5.44 kg)

Body Shape: rounded with full chest and shoulders

Body Structure: short and compact, looks like a fluffy snowball

Coat: soft and silky; 3.5 to 7 inches (8.89 to 17.8 cm) long; multi-layered

Coat Color: ruby-eyed white, pointed white, self, shaded, agouti, broken, smoke, blue, golden, chocolate and lilac

Lifespan: average 7 to 12 years

3.) History of Angora Rabbits as Pets

The details of the Angora Rabbit's history are largely debated but the origins of the breed can be traced back to the 18th century in Ankara, Turkey. It is commonly thought that sailors stopping in Ankara noticed the silky shawls worn by the natives and discovered that the fur was harvested from wooly rabbits. Upon leaving Ankara, the sailors took several of the rabbits back to France – the first appearance of this breed in France is marked in the Encyclopedia for 1765.

The Angora Rabbit first came to the United States during the 1920s and a small commercial industry came into development. The industry never reached the same level it had reached in France however, due to the intense labor required for the business. As a result, Angora Rabbits in the U.S.A. became more popular for show than for wool production.

Over the years, several variations of the Angora Breed came into existence. In 1932 the National Angora Rabbit Breeders

Club (NARBC) was formed as the first specialty club for the breed in the U.S.A. In 1944, the breed was differentiated into two varieties – the English and the French Angora. Before this differentiation, these rabbits were simply shown under the name "Angora Woolers". In 1987, the Satin Angora breed was accepted followed by the Giant Angora in 1988. Today, each breed has its own separate standard but they all belong to the same national club, the NARBC.

a.) History of the ARBA

The American Rabbit Breeders' Association (ARBA) was founded in 1910 and has its headquarters in Bloomington, Illinois. The purpose of this association is to promote rabbit fancy and to facilitate commercial rabbit production. The ARBA is responsible for setting breed standards and sanctioning rabbit shows throughout North America. In addition to sponsoring local clubs and fairs, the ARBA holds a national convention show annually, drawing rabbit fanciers from around the globe.

Not only does the ARBA set breed standards and organize shows, it also serves to provide rabbit raising education. Every five years the ARBA publishes a detailed guide for rabbit fanciers called Standard of Perfection. The ARBA also publishes educational materials like guidebooks and posters including photographs of all the recognized rabbit breeds. Additionally, the ARBA has a library of over 10,000 books and writings on domestic rabbits – the largest single repository of its kind.

b.) History of the BRC

The breeding and showing of rabbits began over two hundred years ago. Throughout the nineteenth century, fanciers gathered to form local clubs for showing and improving individual breeds. The number of rabbit breeds recognized increased throughout the 1800s and early 1900s but by 1918, the most popular breed by far was the Beveren. In May of 1918 breeders of Beveren rabbits gathered to form a national club called The Beveren Club.

The Beveren Club served to raise the profile of rabbit breeding, adopting and standardizing new breeds. Eventually, the name of the club changed to the British Fur Rabbit Society and then to the British Rabbit Society. By 1928, over a dozen different breeds were recognized and interest in rabbit breeding began to grow. As a result, a new club was formed called the National Rabbit Council of Great Britain. The club grew quickly but conflicts arose between the two clubs which led to them eventually merging in 1934 to form the British Rabbit Council.

c.) Angora Rabbit Breed Clubs

Breed clubs are an excellent resource to find information regarding the care and keeping of pet rabbits. In this section you will find some details on rabbit clubs – regional, national and international – devoted specifically to the Angora Rabbit breed. These are great resources for finding out further information about local breeders as well as rabbit shows.

National Angora Club of Great Britain

www.nationalangoraclub.webs.com

The National Angora Club of Great Britain was founded in 1963 as an amalgamation of the British Angora Rabbit Society (BARS) and the United Angora Rabbit Club (UARC). This club serves to support breeders and enthusiasts for the Angora breed putting on annual shows and attending events such as Woolfest.

International Association of German Angora Rabbit Breeders (IAGARB)

www.iagarb.com/germangiant.html

The International Association of German Angora Rabbit Breeders is a club based in North America dedicated to promoting and improving the German Angora Rabbit breed. This club publishes a quarterly newsletter which includes club news and articles related to the care of the German Angora breed.

National Angora Rabbit Breeders Club (NARBC)

www.nationalangorarabbitbreeders.com

The National Angora Rabbit Breeders Club which is based in the Missouri was first recognized in 1932 as a specialty club for the Angora Rabbit breed. It is the goal of the NARBC to promote and improve the Angora Rabbit breed and to provide breeders and enthusiasts with information to advance the interests of the breed and the public.

United Angora Rabbit Club (UARC)

www.unitedangorarabbitclub.org

The United Angora Rabbit Club based in Pennsylvania was chartered in 2007 as a club of Angora rabbit fanciers of all kinds. The club is run for its members, by its members to promote the Angora breed in hopes of one day hosting Angora Nationals.

Southern Angora Rabbit Club (SARC)

http://southernangorarc.weebly.com/

The Southern Angora Rabbit Club is based in Texas and exists to provide support and resources for breeders and lovers of the Angora Rabbit breed. This club sponsors specialty shows, 4-H workshops and judge's conferences among other events.

Appalachian Angora Rabbit Club (AARC)

www.appalachianangoras.org

This club is devoted to promoting the Angora Rabbit breed throughout the Appalachian region and is based in Virginia. The AARC is very active in sponsoring Angora specialty shows and participating in local festivals to educate the public about Angora wool and the animals it comes from.

California Angora Rabbit Society (CARS)

https://groups.yahoo.com/neo/groups/CaliforniaAngoraRabbitSociety/info

This club is made up of individuals who share a passion for spinning, knitting and weaving Angora fiber. Though many members of the club are Angora owners themselves, non-owners are welcomed.

Northern California Angora Guild (NCAG)

http://ncag.blogspot.com

Located in Morgan Hill, California, this guild is open to all rabbit lovers but is particularly devoted to the Angora Rabbit breed. The NCAG participates in local shows and provides support for its members.

Mid-America Angora Club

https://angorarabbit.com/maac

This ARBA chartered club is a non-profit organization that serves Angora Rabbit breeder and fanciers living in Illinois, Kansas and Missouri. The MAAC holds several specialty shows each year and welcomes members from other states.

4.) Types of Angora Rabbits

The American Rabbit Breeders Association (ARBA) recognizes four different breeds of Angora Rabbit: English, French, Giant and Satin. The fifth breed of Angora is the German Angora. Though it is not officially recognized by the ARBA, it is still a fairly popular breed and has its own association called the International Association of German Angora Breeders (IAGARB).

English Angora

The English Angora breed is smaller than the others and one of the most popular breeds to keep as a pet. English Angoras typically weigh about 4.5 to 8 lbs. (2.04 to 3.63 kg) and they are known for their puppy-like facial features.

As long as their coats are properly maintained, grooming of this breed is fairly easy – they need to be groomed about twice per week. Though a variety of colors can be exhibited by English Angoras, only solid colors are accepted by the ARBA. Pure white is the preferred color, but other colors such as golden, cream and sable are possible. The English Angora is the only rabbit breed that has hair completely covering its eyes.

French Angora

The French Angora is slightly larger than the English Angora, weighing between 7.5 and 10 lbs. (3.4 to 4.54 kg) at maturity. These rabbits have a very thick undercoat and a commercial body type. What differentiates this breed from the others is the short hair on its face – it may however, have tufting on the ears or hind legs. The coloring of French Angoras is determined by the color of the fur on the head, feet and tail. Pure white color is preferred, but agouti, shaded, ticked and banded patterns are also accepted.

German Angora

The average size of a German Angora rabbit ranges from about 4.5 to 12 lbs. (2.04 to 5.44 kg). This breed is fairly common in the U.S.A. and Canada but it is not recognized by the ARBA. What sets these rabbits apart is that they are incapable of shedding their coats – they must be sheared.

In most cases, German Angoras are white or albino, though other colors are accepted by the IAGARB. It is not uncommon for breeders to cross German Angoras with other Angora breeds to achieve the dense German-type wool but to eliminate matting.

Giant Angora

As the name suggests, the Giant Angora is the largest Angora breed accepted by the ARBA. This breed reaches a weight of 12 lbs. (5.44 kg) or more at maturity and its coat contains three types of wool – a soft under wool, awn fluff which is the soft crimped fibers ending in a straight tip and awn hair which is strong, straight guard hair protruding above the undercoat. These rabbits have furnishings on the face and ears, but their eyes are not fully covered with fur like the English Angora.

The only color officially accepted by the ARBA for the Giant Angora is ruby-eyed white. Because their hair is the longest of the Angora breeds (grows 1 inch or 2.54 cm per month), this breed is especially prone to wool block which is where a ball of hair forms in the stomach and intestines of the rabbit, preventing it from digesting any food. Please refer to Chapter Seven which gives more information regarding Wool Block and ways to prevent it.

Satin Angora

The Satin Angora is about the same size as the French Angora, weighing between 7 and 10 lbs. (3.18 to 4.54 kg) at maturity. These rabbits are named for the sheen of their wool – the hair shaft is semi-transparent on the outer shell which reflects light. This gives the Satin Angora's coat a deeper color with high luster and a soft texture. Similar in appearance to the French Angora, the Satin Angora has no furnishings on its face. Compared to the English Angora, it is easier to groom but its coat is prone to matting so it requires daily combing.

5.) Colors of Angora Rabbits

As it has already been mentioned, different types of Angora Rabbit may have different colors or patterns but only certain varieties are accepted by the ARBA.

Ruby-Eyed White

The only accepted color for Giant Angora

White overall body color with pink iris and ruby red pupils.

Pointed White

English Angora, French Angora, Satin Angora, German Angora

The body color is clean white with markings in blue, black, chocolate or lilac. Color is only permitted on the nose, ears, feet and tail (referred to as points). Pink iris with red pupils.

Variations: black, blue, chocolate and lilac

Self

English Angora, French Angora, Satin Angora, German Angora

These rabbits exhibit a single, solid color with slightly lighter color wool toward the skin.

Variations: black, blue, chocolate, lilac, white

Shaded

English Angora, French Angora, Satin Angora, German Angora

Variations: *sable, smoke, frosted, tortoiseshell*

Sable

These rabbits have a rich brown coat with guard hairs over the back. The wool on the head, ears, feet and back may be medium to dark sable in color with lighter shading on the chest, flanks, belly and underside of the tail.

Variations: *dark sable*

Smoke Pearl

These rabbits have a dark smoky blue coat with guard hairs over the back. The wool on the head, ears, feet and back is medium smoky blue with lighter pearl gray shading on the chest, belly, flanks and underside of the tail.

Frosted Pearl

These rabbits have a light body color with light or dark markings on the mask, ears, feet and tail.

Variations: *black, blue, chocolate, lilac, sable point*

Tortoiseshell

These rabbits have brown or black color on the face, ears, feet and tail. The wall is typically darker over the back with a smoky shading along the sides, legs and belly.

Variations: *blue, chocolate, lilac*

Agouti

English Angora, French Angora, Satin Angora, German Angora

The body of these rabbits are banded and ticked, the ears laced with color to match the ticking. Most specimens have white or tan circles around the eyes as well as lighter coloration inside the ears, on the neck and on the belly.

Variations: *chestnut, copper, opal, chocolate, lynx, wild gray, chinchilla, squirrel, lilac*

Broken

English Angora, French Angora, German Angora

Pure white coloration on the body plus a blanket pattern or spots in any other angora color (between 10% and 50% of total coat color). Color must be present on both ears, eye circles and nose.

Variations: *chocolate, tortoiseshell, black, lilac, opal, gray, red*

Ticked

French Angora, Satin Angora, German Angora

Solid body color with ticking of tan or silver. Lighter coloration may be present on the belly and underside of the tail. Ermine is a non-showable color resembling a pointed white but having dark tipping on the hairs.

Variations: *steel, silver steel, blue steel, chocolate steel, lilac steel, ermine*

Wide Band

French Angora, Satin Angora, German Angora

Overall body color is fawn, red, cream or ermine. May exhibit a white under-color on the coat as well as lighter coloration around the eyes, inside the ears, under the chin, on the belly and under the tail.

Variations: *fawn, red, cream, ermine*

Chapter Three: What to Know Before You Buy

The Angora Rabbit is not significantly more difficult to care for than other rabbit breeds, but they do have slightly different requirements in terms of feeding, housing and health care. Before you decide to purchase an Angora Rabbit you would be wise to spend a little bit of time learning what to expect from these creatures.

In this chapter you will learn the basics about keeping Angora Rabbits including licensing requirements, keeping them with other pets, initial and monthly costs and even pros and cons of the breed.

1.) Do You Need a License?

Unless you are an experienced rabbit owner, this question probably never occurred to you. It is not uncommon in the U.S.A. and U.K. for a permit to be required to legally keep unusual pets and exotic animals, but does an Angora Rabbit qualify as either of those? It is important that you learn the requirements in your specific area before you buy an Angora Rabbit because if you do not have a permit when it is necessary, you may be subject to hefty fines and may even lose your pet rabbit.

a.) Licensing in the U.S.A.

There is no federal law in the United States of America requiring private rabbit owners to obtain a license for keeping Angora Rabbits. There are, however, certain state laws regarding the keeping and breeding of domestic rabbits. The state of Minnesota, for example, requires rabbit owners to pay a $15 annual fee to license their pet rabbit – a higher fee may be charged if the rabbit is not spayed or neutered.

Generally, retail pet store owners and private collectors are not required to obtain a permit for keeping Angora Rabbits. If you plan to breed your rabbits for wholesale or exhibition, however, you may need to obtain a license. To determine the requirements for your particular area, check with your local council. It is better to be safe than sorry – especially if failing to license your rabbit could cost you hefty fines or you could even lose your pet.

b.) Licensing in the U.K.

The U.K. does not have any legislation requiring rabbit owners or breeders to obtain a license. There are, however, laws in place in regard to importing or exporting animals. Rabies has long been eradicated from the U.K. and strict import and export laws are now in place to prevent the disease from being re-introduced. If you plan to bring a rabbit with you to the U.K., or if you plan to export one, you will need to obtain an animal movement license (AML).

c.) Licensing Elsewhere

Licensing requirements for Angora Rabbits vary from one country or region to another. One of the only cases in which the ownership of pet rabbits is expressly prohibited is in Queensland, Australia. Rabbits are not a native species in Queensland – they are actually considered a Class 2 pest by the Land Protection Act of 2002. A penalty of Australian $44,000 can be levied as a result of flaunting this law.

As they are not a native species, rabbits can threaten the survival of certain native species and also cause damage to the environment. You cannot obtain a license to keep a pet rabbit in Queensland because it is illegal. The only time in which a permit may be issued is if the rabbit is being used for research or entertainment purposes.

2.) How Many Should You Buy?

The number of Angora Rabbits you purchase depends upon the reason for which you are keeping them. If you are only planning to keep your rabbit as a pet, you may only need to purchase one or two. In performing research online, you may find varying opinions regarding whether rabbits are best kept alone or in pairs/groups. The Angora Rabbit is a fairly playful and social breed, so these rabbits in particular tend to do well with others of their own kind.

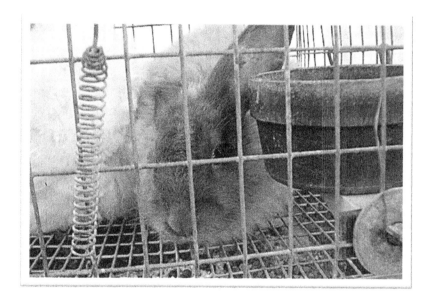

If you are planning on raising Angora Rabbits for their wool, you may need more than just one or two rabbits. Giant Angora Rabbits are the most common breed for production of commercial wool because they produce about 2.2 to 3.3 lbs. (1 to 1.5 kg) wool per year. An English or French Angora Rabbit may produce only half as much wool on a yearly basis. If you plan to spin wool for your own personal use, you may only need a few rabbits to produce enough wool. For commercial producers, however, the more rabbits you are able to keep (without compromising their health or well-being), the better.

3.) Can Angora Rabbits Be Kept with Other Pets?

Though most commonly known for their long fur, Angora Rabbits are also chosen for their loving personalities. Angora Rabbits can form very close bonds with their owners and they even enjoy the company of other rabbits. It is also possible for Angora Rabbits to get along with other house pets including cats and dogs as long as the pets are gentle and well-mannered.

It is not unheard of for an Angora Rabbit to snuggle up next to a friendly cat for an afternoon nap. If you do plan to keep Angora Rabbits in the presence of other pets, be sure to supervise all of the time the animals spend together to avoid accidents. While your other pets may not be aggressive by nature, animal behavior is difficult to predict and it is always better to be safe than sorry.

A word of caution in respect of ferrets which are predatory animals and may injure your rabbit and birds which depending on the species could irritate your rabbit due to their sensitive ears. If you have pets kept in tanks (e. g. fish and frogs), please ensure that your rabbit does not chew on electrical cords. This would obviously apply to any electrical cords throughout your home. My best advice is not to take any chances but ultimately you must make a judgment call as you are best placed to know the character of your pets.

4.) Ease and Cost of Care

As mentioned earlier, the challenge of owning an Angora Rabbit is not significantly larger than that of caring for any other rabbit. There are, however, a few additional considerations to make. One of these is the size of the rabbit – Angoras are much larger than many popular pet breeds including the Netherland Dwarf, Holland Lops and Mini Lops. This being the case, you will need a larger cage or pen for your Angora Rabbit than you would for a smaller breed.

Another thing to consider with Angora Rabbits is that their wooly coats require regular grooming. In most cases, twice-weekly brushing or combing is sufficient but if you plan to show your rabbit you may need to do a little extra work. This affects not only the ease of keeping this breed and the time involved but also the cost because you may need to purchase additional grooming supplies to handle the Angora's thick coat.

In this section you will learn the basic costs you can expect when keeping an Angora Rabbit as a pet. Not only do you need to think about the initial cost of buying your rabbit and its habitat, but you also need to think about the monthly costs to keep the rabbit. These overheads will include food, bedding, chew toys and even cage repairs.

a.) Initial Costs

The initial costs for keeping an Angora Rabbit as a pet include, of course, the purchase price of the rabbit and the cost of the enclosure. The purchase price may vary depending where you get your rabbit and what breed you choose – it will also depend whether you get one or more rabbits. Another significant cost to prepare for is the cost of the habitat – because Angora Rabbits are larger than some rabbit breeds, you will need to budget a little more for this purchase. Other initial costs for Angora Rabbits include: spay/ neuter, microchipping, vaccinations and cage accessories including food bowls and toys.

Purchase Price: The price of an Angora Rabbit will vary depending where you buy it. You may be able to find these rabbits at your local pet store or you can purchase them from a reputable breeder for around $50 to $100 (£32.50 to £65).

Spay/Neuter: If you do not plan to breed your rabbits, it is normally a good idea to spay or neuter them. The cost of the spay/neuter surgery is generally around $100 (£65) but you may be able to find a lower price if there is a veterinary clinic in your area. Seek advice from your vet on the pros and cons of having your rabbit spayed or neutered.

Microchipping: A microchip is a tiny electronic device that is inserted under your rabbit's skin. This device is used to store your contact information so if the rabbit is lost, you can be contacted. It is not a requirement that you have your rabbit microchipped, but it is certainly a good idea. The cost of this procedure is generally about $30 (£19.50).

Vaccinations: One of the first things you need to do when you get a new rabbit is to have it examined by a veterinarian and caught up on its vaccinations. Costs for veterinary care may vary depending where you live but the average cost for initial vaccinations is around $50 (£32.50). The recommended vaccinations will also depend on where you live.

Cage: Angora Rabbits are not a small breed so they need a considerable amount of space, especially if you plan to keep more than one rabbit in the cage. It is always a good idea to keep the motto "bigger is better" in mind when purchasing a cage for Angora Rabbits because it is much better to have more space than your rabbit needs than not to have enough. The cost for an Angora Rabbit's cage will vary depending on size and materials but you should be ready to spend around $200 to $300 (£130 to £195).

Accessories: To prepare your rabbit's cage you will need to stock up on a few accessories. These accessories might include a water bottle, food bowl, bedding and chew toys for your rabbit. Another add-on that would be good to have around is a travel carrier – this will be useful when you need to take your rabbit to the vet. The cost of initial accessories may be around $100 (£65).

Additional Costs: In addition to purchasing your rabbit as well as his cage and accessories, there are a few additional costs you should be prepared for. Some of these costs might include a litter pan, grooming supplies and cleaning equipment. For the most part, these tools and supplies should last you for several years and the total cost may average around $100 (£65).

Summary of Initial Costs

Cost Type	One Rabbit	Two Rabbits
Purchase Price	$50 to $100 (£32.50 to £65)	$100 to $200(£65 to £130)
Spay/Neuter	$100 (£65)	$200 (£130)
Microchipping	$30 (£19.50)	$60 (£39)
Vaccinations	$50 (£32.50)	$100 (£65)
Cage or Pen	$200 to $300 (£130 to £195)	$200 to $300 (£130 to £195)
Cage Accessories	$100 (£65)	$100 (£65)
Other Tools/Equipment	$100 (£65)	$100 (£65)
Total:	$630 to $780 (£409.50 to £507)	$860 to $1,060 (£559 to £689)

b.) Monthly Costs

The initial costs for purchasing an Angora Rabbit and the necessary supplies may range from $630 to $780 (£409.50 to £507) for one rabbit and from $860 to $1,060 (£559 to £689) for two rabbits. These costs are fairly significant but you also need to think about the monthly cost of maintaining your Angora Rabbit. Some of the monthly expenditures you should anticipate include food, bedding, veterinary care, replacement toys and perhaps even repairs to the cage. Unless you are able to meet these monthly expenses in addition to the initial costs for an Angora Rabbit you may want to consider a different pet.

Food: Your monthly costs for rabbit food will vary depending how many rabbits you keep and what type of food you buy. Some of the types of food you will need to buy for your rabbits include greens, hay, commercial rabbit pellets and fresh vegetables. The budget to feed a single Angora Rabbit for one month averages at about $50 to $75 (£32.50 to £48.75).

Bedding: No matter where you keep you rabbit whether in its cage or hutch, or if you are relaxed and have him roam free throughout the house, you will need to provide him a 'safe' place he can call his own. In terms of bedding, the best kinds to use are non-toxic pelleted litter, fresh hay or newspaper. Pine and cedar shavings can cause irritation and both clay and clumping cat litters can be harmful to rabbits.

Your monthly cost for bedding will also depend on the type of bedding you buy. In general, you should plan to spend up to $20 (£13) per month on bedding. You can reduce your bedding costs by using recycled newspapers, but do not use colored magazines because the ink may contain toxins that are harmful to your rabbit if he eats it. No matter what type of bedding you choose, be sure to replace it often even if it doesn't look like it needs it.

Veterinary Care: If you care for your Angora Rabbit properly, you should not have to worry about veterinary care on a monthly basis. You should, however, take your rabbit to the vet for a check-up once a year. The total yearly cost for this is generally around $50 (£32.50) which is less than $5 (£3.25) per month. However, you cannot predict veterinary expenses if your rabbit becomes unexpectedly ill and should have savings for this or could consider pet insurance. Please see Chapter Seven for more details.

Additional Costs: Other monthly costs you should be prepared for include replacing chew toys and making repairs to the cage or supplies. These outlays are generally not very high and may only be $60 (£39) per year which is $5 (£3.25) per month.

Summary of Monthly Costs

Cost Type	One Rabbit	Two Rabbits
Food	$50 to $75 (£32.50 - £48.75)	$100 to $150 (£65 - £97.50)
Bedding	$50 (£32.50)	$50 (£32.50)
Veterinary Care	$5 (£3.25)	$10 (£6.50)
Additional Costs	$5 (£3.25)	$10 (£6.50)
Total:	$110 to $135 (£71.50 - £87.75)	$170 to $220 (£110.50 - £143)

c.) Time Considerations

In addition to the initial and monthly costs for keeping Angora Rabbits, you also need to think about the amount of care these animals require. Though Angora Rabbits are not difficult to keep as pets, they do require regular maintenance.

Refer to the following lists to get an idea how much time you will need to dedicate to your rabbit's care on a daily and weekly basis. These are of course just a guide. It depends on whether you are keeping your Angora Rabbit as a pet or for its wool.

Daily Tasks to Complete:

- Clean food dish and refresh food
- Clean water bottle and refresh water
- Moving rabbit to exercise pen (20 to 30 minutes daily)
- Interacting with the rabbit
- Observation/basic health check
- Combing/brushing rabbit (may not be necessary every day, but multiple times per week)

Estimated Daily Commitment: 1 hour

Weekly Tasks to Complete:

- Completely replacing bedding
- Cleaning out cage and accessories

- More detailed health check
- Spending extended time interacting with rabbit
- Checking ears, nails and teeth

Estimated Weekly Commitment: 10 hours

5.) Pros and Cons of Angora Rabbits

As is true of any pet, the Angora Rabbit has its pros and cons. Before you purchase one, you should take the time to weigh the advantages and disadvantages of this breed to determine whether it is really the right animal for you. If, having read this section, you feel that the Angora Rabbit is the right choice for you, we can move on to the next chapter where we look at what to consider when making a purchase.

Pros for Angora Rabbits:

- Very friendly breed, can be very social
- Can get along with other household pets
- Forms close bonds with owners
- Can be kept with other rabbits in the same cage
- Produces long, soft wool that can be spun into yarn
- Five different breeds to choose from

- Coat is fairly easy to maintain with regular grooming

- Very beautiful breed, long and luxurious coat

- Unique appearance, will get lots of attention

- Can be litter trained – makes it easier to clean up after them, especially indoor rabbits

- Angora wool doesn't have the same allergy-causing qualities as other pet fur

Cons for Angora Rabbits:

- Some breeds get very large and require significant space

- Coats require regular grooming (at least twice-weekly brushing)

- May not do well without regular human interaction (best not to be left alone for long periods)

- Prone to developing wool block which can become fatal

- May not do well in extreme heat – best kept indoors

- Cage should be cleaned often to prevent odor

- Free-roaming rabbits may chew on furniture or power cords

6.) Human Health Considerations

Before you buy, you also need to consider any implications to your and your families own health. For example, do you know if you have an allergy or sensitivity to rabbits? I would recommend taking advice from your Doctor to ensure that you understand the implications to your own health and if necessary, are allergy tested.

Chapter Four: Purchasing Angora Rabbits

After reading the first few chapters of this book, you should have a good idea whether an Angora Rabbit is the right breed for you. Once you have made this decision you can move on to thinking about purchasing an Angora Rabbit.

There are several ways to go about buying a pet rabbit but the best way is typically to buy from a breeder. Rabbit breeders have more knowledge and experience with the breed than your average pet store worker, so you are more likely to receive a well-bred and healthy rabbit from a reputable source.

1.) Where to Buy Angora Rabbits

When it comes to buying Angora Rabbits, you have several options to choose from. Because this breed is not one of the most common rabbit breeds you may not be able to find them in your local pet store in any event. If you plan to breed your rabbits or train them for show, you should plan to purchase from an independent breeder anyway. For those who simply want an Angora Rabbit as a pet, another excellent option is to adopt a rabbit from your local rabbit rescue group.

a.) Buying in the U.S.A.

You should not expect to be able to walk into your local pet store and find an Angora Rabbit. They will probably stock some of the more common breeds of domestic rabbit, but they will see this breed as a bit of an exotic. Even if the pet store does have some available, you should not necessarily buy one without shopping around first. In buying from a pet store, you do not necessarily know where the rabbit came from and unlikely that they will have any information about its genetics and family history.

The safest option for finding an Angora Rabbit is to go to a breeder. This way your rabbit will be less likely to get sick or have temperament problems. You also have the comfort of knowing that you have an expert you can call on if you have any questions, or if you run into problems with your rabbit.

You can find local breeders by performing an online search or if you are feeling cheeky, you can ask your local pet store or better still your local veterinarian for a referral. Once you find a breeder, make sure you ask plenty of questions to ascertain the breeder's experience and to ensure that the rabbit you bring home is healthy. A good breeder will also want to ensure you are the right owner for one of its rabbits and will no doubt want to satisfy themselves that you are fully aware of the commitment and responsibility you are taking on.

Another option is to perform an online search for Angora Rabbit breeders. You can often find listings of breeders on national websites such as the American Rabbit Breeders Association (ARBA). If all else fails, look for a rabbit rescue in your area. You may not find a rescue that has baby rabbits available, but adult rabbits are likely to already be litter trained and are more likely to be caught up on vaccinations. If you want a pet, it is great to be able to give a rescue rabbit a good home.

United States of America Websites for Angora Breeders and Suppliers:

French Angora Rabbits,
https://angorarabbit.com/hutch/weblinks.php?cat_id=5

Giant Angora Rabbits,
https://angorarabbit.com/hutch/weblinks.php?cat_id=7

Satin Angora Rabbits,
https://angorarabbit.com/hutch/weblinks.php?cat_id=6

German Angora Rabbits,
https://angorarabbit.com/hutch/weblinks.php?cat_id=8

English Angora Rabbits,
https://angorarabbit.com/hutch/weblinks.php?cat_id=4

Member List National Angora Rabbit Breeders Club
(NARBC),
www.nationalangorarabbitbreeders.com/member-list.htm

RabbitBreeders.us,
http://rabbitbreeders.us/english-angora-rabbit-breeders

ARBA Breeder Listing,
www.arba.net/breeders.htm

United States of America Rabbit Rescues:

The Rabbit Haven Adoption Showcase,
www.therabbithaven.org/adoption_showcase.htm

RightPet Angora Rescue Listing, www.rightpet.com/small-exotic-mammalrescues/adoption-rescue/giant-angora-rabbit/all

b.) Buying in the U.K.

The options for buying a Flemish Giant Rabbit in the UK
are fairly similar to the U.S. Again, you are unlikely to find
one for sale at your local pet store, but there are of course
exceptions but my guidance as to its origin, genetics and
family background still apply. Shop around a bit and take
the time to find some local breeders as this should prove
the better option long term.

If you don't want to buy from a pet store, ask your
veterinarian or fellow rabbit owners for a referral to a

breeder. Another option is to check the breeder listings on the British Rabbit Council or National Angora Club of Great Britain websites.

United Kingdom Websites for Angora Breeders and Suppliers:

RabbitBreeders.org.uk
http://rabbitbreeders.org.uk/angora-rabbit-breeders

Don's Angoras
www.angoras.co.uk/wordpress

National Angora Club of Great Britain,
http://nationalangoraclub.webs.com/

The British Rabbit Council (BRC) Breeders Directory
www.thebrc.org/breeders-list.htm

Again, in the UK adopting from a local rabbit rescue is also another option. If you are interested in this as a possibility, try some of these resources to find one:

The Rabbit Residence Rescue.
www.rabbitresidence.org.uk

Cotton Tails Rescue.
http://cottontails-rescue.org.uk

Rabbit Rehome.
www.rabbitrehome.org.uk/breeds.asp

PreLoved,
www.preloved.co.uk/adverts/list/3659/rabbits.html?keyword=angora

2.) How to Select a Healthy Angora Rabbit

Unfortunately, many inexperienced rabbit owners make the mistake of purchasing an Angora Rabbit without first gauging its health level. Once you purchase a rabbit you may not be able to return it if you find out it has health problems – by that point, you are likely to have already bonded with the rabbit and will be reluctant to return it anyway.

Do not be tempted to think that you are doing the rabbit a kindness by taking home a rabbit that has obvious health issues – it will just be a lot of headache and heartache for you in the long run and the rabbit may not even live very long. Do yourself a favor and take the time to make sure that the Angora Rabbit you bring home is in good condition.

Follow these tips to bring home a healthy Angora Rabbit:

1. Do your research before picking a breeder and buying a rabbit

2. Take a tour of the facilities

3. Observe and examine the rabbit kits individually

4. Make your choice and start the process

Do your research: Shop around for a reputable breeder and take the time to interview each breeder. Ask questions to ascertain the breeder's knowledge of and experience with the Angora Breed. If the breeder can't answer your questions or appears to be avoiding them, move on to another breeder.

Ask for a tour: Once you select a breeder, it is always a good idea to pay a visit to the facilities. Ask to see the places where the rabbits are kept and ask to see the parents of the litter from which you are buying. If the facilities are dirty or the parents appear to be in poor health, do not purchase a rabbit from that breeder, thank them for their time and move on.

Observe the kits: If the facilities and parents appear to be in good order, ask to see the litter of rabbits. Observe their appearance and activity to see if they look healthy. Healthy Angora Rabbits should be active and curious, not hiding in a corner or looking lethargic.

Examine the rabbits individually: If the litter appears to be in good condition, pick out a few of the rabbits that you like. Handle the rabbits briefly to see how they react to human interaction and check them for obvious signs of disease and injury. Check the rabbit's ears and nose for discharge and make sure that the eyes are bright and clear. The rabbit's teeth should be straight and its coat healthy. In Angora Rabbits, the coat should feel very soft and silky – if it is matted or coarse, it could be a sign of ill health.

If, after touring the facilities and ensuring that the rabbits themselves are healthy, you can begin to make negotiations with the breeder. Make sure you get the rabbit's medical history and breeding information for your own records. Ask if the rabbit comes with a health guarantee and make sure you get all the paperwork necessary to register your rabbit, should you choose to do so. A good breeder is someone to keep in touch with, for if you have any concerns or worries, they are generally only too delighted to pass on their wisdom and knowledge. They will love their rabbits and will be delighted that you are a caring and interested enough to go back to them for advice.

Chapter Five: Caring for Angora Rabbits

If you have never owned a pet rabbit before, you may be tempted to think that it will be "easier" than caring for a cat or dog. In reality, Angora Rabbits require just as much care as any other pet. The level of care you provide for your Angora will have a direct effect on its health and well-being.

In this chapter you will learn a wealth of information that you need to know in order to provide your Angora Rabbit with a proper habitat and healthy diet. I also cover litter training, grooming and a brief look at harvesting its wool.

1.) Habitat Requirements

Before you bring home an Angora Rabbit you need to be sure you have a proper habitat set up. If you do not provide your rabbit with a large enough cage that provides shelter and comfort, your rabbit is less likely to thrive. If you plan to use your Angora Rabbit for its fur, you should also know that if your rabbit is not happy or healthy, the quality of its fur will decline. In this section you will learn the basics of creating the ideal habitat for your pet Angora Rabbit.

a.) General Habitat Requirements

The first thing you need to consider when creating a habitat for your Angora Rabbit is the size of the cage. Angora Rabbits are a fairly large breed so they need a significant amount of space in order to be happy and healthy. A cage should be long enough that your rabbit can make three or four hops from one end to the other. It should be wide enough that your rabbit can stretch out across the width and tall enough that it can stand on its hind legs.

For some of the larger breeds of Angora Rabbit you may want to add a little extra space.

The next thing you need to think about is the construction of the cage. The most popular material for rabbit cages is galvanized welded wire. These cages allow for plenty of ventilation while also providing structure for the cage. Because the walls are made of wire, you do not have to worry about your rabbit consuming toxic paint or plastic. Ideally, the wire should be galvanized after weld and 14 or 16 gauge. If there are any sharp edges inside or outside the cage, they should be filed down and covered with cloth to prevent injury to yourself and your rabbit.

In terms of bedding, the best kinds to use are non-toxic pelleted litter, fresh hay or newspaper. The dyes and inks used in the vast majority of newspapers today are made from soy based inks. Be cautious as pine and cedar shavings can cause irritation and both clay and clumping cat litters can be harmful to rabbits. You should also avoid using colored magazine pages as bedding because the ink on the pages may be toxic – it could be dangerous for your rabbit if he eats it.

One other important thing to consider in regard to your rabbit's cage is its location. Later in this section you will learn the benefits of keeping your rabbits indoors versus outdoors but here we will briefly mention the right location for your Angora's cage indoors. It is important to find a location that is free from drafts or extreme heat – this means you shouldn't place your rabbit's cage right next to a window or a heating/cooling vent. You should also keep the cage out of direct sunlight and out of high-traffic areas. You want to be sure your rabbit gets plenty of attention but if there is too much noise or activity around the cage he may become skittish.

An outdoor open exercise pen or rabbit run can be as large as you like but the walls should be at least 3 feet (91.4 cm) high so your bunny doesn't escape. You may also want to bury the wire at least a few inches underground to prevent him from digging under it. I strongly recommend that you also make sure the top of the pen is covered to prevent predators from having access to attack your rabbit.

Another thing you need to consider when keeping your rabbit in an exercise pen outdoors is covering about half of the pen with a towel or another solid object to provide your rabbit with shade from the sun and shelter from the elements.

b.) Benefits of Different Cage Types

While wire cages are ideal for Angora Rabbits, you are likely to see a number of different cages if you pay a visit to your local pet store. One of the key differences you will notice is the base of the cages – some have wire bases while others are solid metal or plastic. There are benefits to both of these options but also disadvantages. All-wire bottoms, for example, make cleanup easier because droppings fall right through the bottom into a collection tray rather than accumulating in the cage. The downside of wire-bottomed cages is that they can irritate your rabbit's tender feet and so are not recommended.

In visiting your local pet store or researching rabbit cages online, you may also see rabbit cages featuring multiple levels. Angora Rabbits do not necessarily need multi-level cages but they can be a good option if you do not have a great deal of floor space available. Multi-level cages allow you to provide your rabbit with easy exercise by providing ramps to multiple levels. This enables you to increase the square footage of usable space in your cage without taking up much additional floor space in your room – this is especially useful if you are not able to give your rabbit much time outside the cage to exercise.

c.) Keeping Angoras Indoors vs. Outdoors

If you research this topic online you are likely to find varying answers regarding which is best for Angora Rabbits – being kept indoors or outdoors. In the end, it is really your choice but you should take a few minutes to learn the pros and cons of both options. If you plan to keep multiple rabbits, keeping your rabbits outdoors will minimize the odor and won't take up valuable floor space in your home. The major downside of keeping rabbits outdoors is that they can be exposed to extreme weather conditions as well as wild animals and parasites including fleas/ticks.

Angora Rabbits are, however, particularly well adapted to being kept outdoors due to their thick coats. In cool weather, throwing a blanket over the cage will help to keep your rabbit warm. It is also essential that you keep his fur well groomed because if his fur is matted, it will not insulate him from the cold as effectively.

As an alternative to keeping your rabbit outside permanently, you can also consider giving your rabbit an outdoor run or pen. This allows your rabbit to spend some time outside only when the weather and temperature is appropriate. An enclosed open exercise pen or rabbit run can be as large as you like but the walls should be at least 36 inches (91.4 cm) high so your bunny has plenty of room.

If you choose to build an outdoor rabbit run, be sure to bury the wire at least a few inches/centimeters underground to prevent him from digging under it. Please also make sure the top of the pen is covered with for example, wire mesh so that predators cannot get in to attack your rabbit.

It is always recommended that you cover a large area of the pen with a towel or another solid object to provide your rabbit with shade. As always, make sure your rabbit has access to fresh water so he does not become dehydrated.

You also need to keep in mind that extremely hot weather can be dangerous for Angora Rabbits. Some precautions you must take include keeping the hutch well ventilated, providing plenty of water to drink and providing a frozen water bottle for your rabbit to lean against if he gets too hot. As advice about keeping your rabbit outdoors or indoors will vary depending on where you live, it is advisable to take advice from your local veterinarian or breeder. They will also be able to advise you about coping with the weather conditions in your area.

d.) Recommended Cage Accessories

In addition to picking out the ideal cage for your Angora Rabbit, you also need to make sure you include the proper accessories. Some of the basic cage equipment you are likely to need include food dishes and water bottles. Some of the other fittings you might want to consider including are a hay wheel, a litter pan and chew toys. Below you will find an in-depth explanation of the cage accessories recommended for Angora Rabbits:

Food Dishes: There are a wide variety of food dishes to choose from and they can be made from all kinds of materials. Plastic dishes are easy to clean but your rabbit is likely to chew on them so they will need to be replaced over time. If you do buy plastic, be sure it is non-toxic and BPA free. For your rabbit's food pellets, you will need a ceramic dish that doesn't take up too much space in the cage. A ceramic dish is recommended because it is heavy enough that your rabbit won't be likely to knock it over, and it will be easy to keep clean. Stainless steel dishes are preferred by many rabbit owners because they stand up well and are also easy to clean.

Water Receptacles: In most cases, a plastic water bottle (BPA free) is suitable for Angora Rabbits. Depending on how your rabbit was raised, however, he may prefer a water dish. Just remember to keep the receptacle clean and refresh the water on a daily basis.

Hay Wheel: Hay is an important part of a rabbit's diet and there are a number of different ways you can present it. A hay rack or hanging basket keeps the hay off the floor of the cage so it does not become contaminated. A hay wheel is another great option and it does not necessarily need to be affixed to the side of the cage.

Hiding Places: Rabbits are a prey animal, which means that they need hiding places available in the cage to make them feel more secure. Virtually anything can be made into a hiding place for a rabbit as long as it is large enough to accommodate the rabbit's whole body and is high enough that he can duck in quickly. Some potential items to use as hiding places include cardboard boxes, plastic igloos, wooden shelters or small travel carriers. Hiding places should be lined with bedding to make them more comfortable for your rabbit. Just remember the golden rule with all cage accessories to make sure that they are made from non-toxic BPA free materials.

Chew Toys: Chew toys and other toys provide a rabbit with a valuable source of enrichment. The ideal toys for rabbits should give your rabbit an opportunity to exhibit natural behaviors such as digging, jumping and chewing. Chew toys are especially important for rabbits because they will help to keep the teeth filed down so they do not become overgrown or maloccluded. The following materials can be used to make toys for rabbits: paper, cardboard, plastic or fabric tunnels, mirrors, wood, straw/wicker balls, baby toys, etc. Please ensure that any materials used are non-toxic and BPA free.

2.) Feeding Angora Rabbits

Feeding your Angora Rabbit a healthy diet is probably the most important thing you can do for your pet. Without a proper diet, your rabbit may not thrive and the condition of his fur may suffer as well. Like all rabbits, Angora Rabbits require a varied diet of hay, commercial pellets, fresh fruits, vegetables and treats. In this section you will learn about formulating a healthy staple diet and a supplemental diet for your Angora Rabbit.

a.) Basic Nutritional Needs

Though most rabbits require a low protein, high fiber diet, Angora Rabbits actually need a little bit of extra protein. The extra protein in their diet helps these rabbits to develop their thick wool. Generally, Angora Rabbits require a rabbit feed that supplies them with about 18% protein. This should be supplemented with free access to Timothy hay and other roughage as well as occasional fresh fruits and vegetables. Treats should only be offered about once a week but fresh de-chlorinated water should be constantly available and refreshed on a daily basis.

The staple of your rabbit's diet should be some kind of hay or roughage. These foods will provide your rabbit with the fiber it needs as well as other important vitamins and minerals. Timothy hay is the ideal hay to feed Angora Rabbits because it has a healthy ratio of fiber to protein. Other hays like alfalfa hay may be too high in protein which, combined with the higher protein content of the commercial pellets, can irritate your rabbit's stomach.

Other good hays to feed your rabbit include orchard grass and Bermuda grass – check your local feed stores to find good quality hay. The hay should be green and fragrant without signs of dust or mold. Not only is dusty or moldy hay lower in nutritional value, but it can actually harm your rabbit by making him sick. In many cases you can get a large bale of Timothy hay for under $5 (£3.25). Hay should be constantly available to your rabbit, offered through a hay rack or hay wheel for easy access.

Safe Foods

Apples	Orange
Beans	Pear
Blueberries	Papaya
Carrots	Pineapple
Cherries	Peach
Dandelion Greens	Peas
Grapes	Parsnip
Kale	Parsley
Mustard Greens	Raspberries
Mango	Strawberries
Melon	Tomatoes (fruit)

Keep in mind that certain plants can be very harmful for your Angora Rabbit. Before you feed your rabbit anything besides Timothy hay or pellets, you should check the list below or with you vet or breeder:-

Harmful to Rabbits:

Acorns	Juniper
Aloe	Jack-in-the-Pulpit
Apple Seeds	Laurel Lupine
Almonds	Lily of the Valley
Asparagus Fern	Marigold
Azalea	Milkweed
Carnations	Mistletoe
Clematis	Nutmeg
Daffodil Bulbs	Oak
Eucalyptus	Parsnip
Fruit Pits	Poppy
Fruit Seeds	Peony
Geranium	Philodendron
Gladiola	Poinsettia
Hemlock	Rhubarb Leaves
Hyacinth Bulbs	Sweet Potato
Impatiens	Tansy
Iris	Tomato Leaves
Ivy	Tulip Bulbs
Jasmine	Violet
Jessamine	Yew

These lists are not comprehensive; in order to determine whether a specific plant is toxic for your rabbit, consult the House Rabbit Society website: http://rabbit.org/poisonous-plants/

b.) Commercial Rabbit Pellets

Though not the staple of your rabbit's diet, commercial rabbit pellets are still very important. Commercial pellets help to provide your Angora Rabbit with the protein he needs to maintain a healthy coat as well as to fill in the nutritional gaps left by the feeding of hay. When buying commercial rabbit pellets you should be careful not to buy more than 1 month's supply because if the pellets are not fresh, they can make your rabbit sick. You should also be careful about how you store the pellets – storing them in an airtight container will help keep them fresh.

In terms of feeding your rabbit pellets, they will become a less significant part of your rabbit's diet as he grows. Once your rabbit has been weaned, you should make rabbit pellets constantly available to help your rabbit grow. Around 12 weeks of age you should begin to introduce small amounts of fresh vegetables into the diet to supplement the constant access to hay and pellets.

When your rabbit reaches about 7 months of age you should begin to cut back on the amount of pellets you are feeding him on a daily basis. Between the ages of 7 months and 1 year, you should be giving your Angora Rabbit about ½ cup (4 ounces / 115 grams) of pellets per 6 lbs. / 2.72 kg bodyweight.

Once your rabbit passes the 1-year mark you can cut back again, feeding only ¼ to ½ cup 2 to 4 ounces / 57.5 to 115 grams of pellets a day per 6 lbs. / 2.72 kg bodyweight. At this point, you should also begin to incorporate at least 2 cups (4 to 6 ounces / 113 to 170 grams) of fresh veggies per day in your rabbit's diet.

c.) Supplemental Food and Treats

The main source of nutrition for Angora Rabbits should be received from fresh hay and daily rations of commercial pellets.

Fresh vegetables, particularly leafy greens, also play an important role in a rabbit's nutrition. You can feed your rabbit a variety of greens including fresh herbs, pesticide-free weeds, spinach, lettuce and other vegetable greens. Be sure to feed your rabbit a variety of greens on a daily basis, not just one particular type at each feeding.

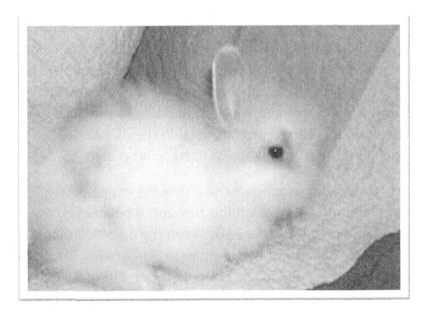

Your rabbit may also enjoy other vegetables including cabbage, broccoli and kale. In addition to leafy greens, you can offer your rabbit fresh fruit or other treats on occasion. Some of the fruits Angora Rabbits enjoy include bananas, apples (remove the seeds), grapes and berries.

You can choose to feed your rabbit a small amount of fruit on a daily basis, but the daily ration should not exceed 2 tablespoons due to the sugar content of the fruit.

Other treats for rabbits may include carrots, sunflower seeds, rolled oats and dried bread. Whenever you incorporate a new treat into your rabbit's diet, do so in very small quantities so as not to upset his stomach.

d.) General Feeding Tips for Rabbits:

- Check your feed often for signs of mold or foul odor – these signs indicate that the feed has gone bad

- Choose a certain time of day to feed your rabbits or divide their food into two daily meals (rabbits appreciate routine)

- Trust your rabbits – if they suddenly stop eating the feed there may be something wrong with it and you should remove it immediately

- If they stop eating and it isn't the food, they may be ill, so watch them carefully and take them to the vet if you are concerned.

- Make any dietary changes slowly – drastic changes in feed can cause severe digestive problems

- Always use pellets within 60 days of manufacture (not purchase)

- Avoid commercially produced rabbit treats because they are rarely healthy

- Always keep an unlimited supply of fresh water available for your rabbits – dehydration can cause severe health problems

3.) Litter Training Your Rabbit

If you have never owned a pet rabbit before, you may be surprised to hear that they can actually be litter trained. Rabbits are creatures of habit by nature, so you simply need to take advantage of this fact in order to train your rabbit to use a litter box. You will need to start by isolating your rabbit in a small area without carpeting (this will make it easier to clean up any mess. It may take a few weeks for your rabbit to begin using the litter box regularly, but it will definitely be worth the effort.

a.) Steps to Litter Training

1. Prepare a litter box using a plastic tub and compressed paper litter – you should also add some fresh hay so your rabbit can munch while using the litter box.

2. Scoop some feces from the cage into the litter box so your rabbit understands what it is to be used for – you can also add a urine-soaked paper towel to add to the scent.

3. Place a small treat like a few sprigs of fresh herbs in the litter box to entice your rabbit to use it.

4. Find the area of the cage where your rabbit tends to prefer to do his business and place the litter box in that area – you may also start

with several litter boxes and remove them as you find your rabbit's favorite.

5.   Limit your rabbit's freedom during training to ensure that he has to use the litter box to do his business.

6.   Clean up any accidents as quickly as possible and, if you catch your rabbit in the act of eliminating outside the litter box, move him to the litter box if you can!

7.   Gradually give your rabbit more space in the pen as he gets used to using the litter box – do not open it up too quickly or he may revert back to old habits.

Keep an eye on your rabbit and take note of which areas he tends to choose to do his business. Keep the litter boxes in those areas and remove the rest. Your rabbit might have a few accidents outside the litter box now and then but this is normal behavior.

**Note: Certain types of litter are harmful to Angora Rabbits including clay litter, clumping litter, pine or cedar shavings and corn cob litter.

4.) Tips for Grooming Angoras

You will need to groom your Angora Rabbit regularly whether you plan to use the wool or not. Ideally, you will make it part of your daily routine "cuddle session" to remove loose fur. Grooming an Angora Rabbit is not necessarily difficult, but you do need a few supplies and some basic information regarding how it is best done. For the most part, Angora grooming can be accomplished using dog grooming tools – you will need a steel-toothed comb, a slicker brush, a bristle brush and a pair of scissors to cut out mats.

The minimum frequency with which you should groom your rabbit is once per week. If you brush or comb him more often, it will help to prevent matting and will improve the condition of his coat. Keep in mind that Angora Rabbits shed every two to three months (this is also called molting) so you will need to groom your rabbit more during these times to control the shedding. During shedding periods you may need to actually pluck bits of loose fur out of the rabbit's coat when you see them trailing off his back.

a.) Step-by-Step Grooming Guide

I've listed below a simple step-by-step guide for grooming.

1. Place your rabbit on a flat table – if your rabbit is skittish, you can also place him on your lap.

2. Use a slicker brush or bristle brush to remove loose hairs from your rabbit's coat – work the brush gently through the rabbit's coat in the direction of hair growth.

3. Start on your rabbit's head at the base of his ears and brush the fur on the back of his neck.

4. Work down the rabbit's back, continuing to move in the direction of hair growth, until you reach his rump.

5. Brush the fur on your rabbit's legs, moving in the direction of hair growth.

6. Roll the rabbit over onto its back to get the stomach and inside of the legs with the brush.

7. If you encounter a mat in your rabbit's fur, work through it gently using a wide-toothed comb.

8. If you cannot work the mat out, cut it out using the scissors -- when cutting out a mat, pinch the fur as close to the skin as possible and cut the mat away above your fingers – this will keep you from accidentally cutting your rabbit.

For more detailed information on grooming, please have a look at this website: -
http://bettychuenglishangora.com/grooming/

If you plan to harvest the wool from your rabbit you will need to do so when the rabbit molts – this happens every two to three months. There are two options for harvesting wool – you can pluck it by hand or shear it using a pair of electric clippers.

German Angoras do not molt like the other breeds so you will need to use a pair of clippers on these rabbits in any event. For the other breeds, however, hand-plucking is a common practice.

b.) Steps for Hand-Plucking

To hand-pluck your rabbit's coat, all you need to do is wait until you start to see loose fibers coming off the rabbit's back and collecting on the cage floor. At this point, you will know that your rabbit's coat is ready to be plucked.

1. First, groom your rabbit to remove any mats from his coat – it will also make is easier to pluck the fur.

2. Carefully flip your rabbit over onto his stomach and begin plucking the fur there – be careful because the skin on your rabbit's belly may be tender.

3. Grasp a small section of fur in your fingers and gently pull the long fur away from your rabbit's body.

4. Work in one small section at a time so you can see where you have already plucked.

5. Gather the plucked fur in a paper bag as you go.

6. Once you finish the fur on the belly, move on to the fur on your rabbit's legs and back.

c.) Steps for Shearing Wool

Shearing is a better option for certain type of Angora Rabbit including the Giant Angora and the Satin Angora. I've listed below a step-by-step guide for shearing your Angora Rabbit's wool:

1. Wait until your rabbit is at least 5 months old (closer to 7 or 8 months for Giant Angora Rabbits) – the section of wool you plan to shear should be at least 3 to 4 inches long.

2. Make sure the blades of your shears are sharp so they do not snag or tug at the coat.

3. Place your rabbit on a table or flat surface and use a comb to make a part down the center of the rabbit's back.

4. Take a small section of wool at the base of your rabbit's neck between your thumb and forefinger.

5. Open the scissors and cut through the section of wool at an angle – this will help to ensure that you don't accidentally cut your rabbit's skin.

6. Repeat the process, moving down your rabbit's back and legs.

7. Carefully flip your rabbit onto his back and shear the stomach as described above.

8. Continue to shear your rabbit once every four months or so, as needed.

If you plan to sell your rabbit's wool, store it in between sheets of tissue paper in a box, making sure the clumps of wool are all facing the same direction. If you plan to spin the wool yourself, you should wait until it grows at least 3 to 4 inches (7.62 to 10.2 cm) long.

d.) Spinning Angora Wool

What makes Angora Rabbit wool so unique is the fact that you can spin it directly from the rabbit – it does not necessarily need to be cleaned or carded before you spin. If you have never spun wool before, however, you may find it easier to pluck or shear the wool from the rabbit first. For the best results, use a cotton carder that has very fine teeth. A cotton carder is a type of brush used to prepare wool for spinning – you will use a pair of hand cards, brushing the wool between the two to make it smooth. Below is a list of steps for carding Angora wool:

1. Place a section of harvested Angora fiber on one of the carders with the end of the section hanging off.

2. Hold the carder with the wool on it in one hand and the second carder in your other hand.

3. Sandwich the two carders together with the handles both facing in the same direction.

4. Carefully brush the wool, holding one carder steady and using the other to work through the wool until smooth.

5. If you groom the rabbit before harvesting, you shouldn't have too many mats – if you do encounter a mat, simply keep brushing until it works out.

6. Continue to brush the wool until all of the fibers are running in the same direction.

7. Remove the wool from the carders and place it in between sheets of tissue paper until you are ready to spin it.

8. Repeat the process with the rest of your wool, working in small batches.

Once you have carded your Angora wool, it should be ready for spinning. Keep in mind that Angora Rabbit wool is very fine and slippery, so it can be more difficult to spin than other types of wool. Be prepared to make some mistakes the first few times you try and realize that you will get better at it with practice.

The best way to spin Angora wool is by hand with a top whorl spindle. The spindle itself should be very lightweight and it should be spun with little tension at high speed for the best results. Follow the steps below to spin your Angora wool into yarn:

1. Gather the carded wool and gently pull at it to create a length of "roving" at least 12 inches long.

2. Carefully wrap the length of roving around your non-dominant wrist (keep it fairly loose), leaving several inches on the end free.

3. Tie the leader (a 12-inch strand of yarn) to the top of your spindle if one is not already attached.

4. Pinch the end of the roving together with the end of the leader with your non-dominant hand.

5. Give the spindle a good clockwise spin and let it hang as the leader and the wool twist together.

6. Once the twist has built up on the leader, stop the spindle between your knees.

7. Pinch the leader and fiber together at the end of the twist and release another few inches of roving from your wrist.

8. Release the pinched section, allowing the twist to move into the new section of roving.

9. Repeat this process, spinning the spindle in a clockwise direction and slowly adding more of the roving to the growing length of yarn.

You may find that the amount of tension you place on the leader affects the thickness of the yarn – feel free to experiment until you find a thickness that you like. Once you have a good length of yarn finished, you may want to wrap it around the shaft of your spindle to keep it out of your way as you keep spinning. If you do this, leave about 10 inches of the yarn free.

For more detailed information on grooming, please have a look at these websites: -

http://joyofhandspinning.com/how-to-care-for-your-angora-rabbit

http://leighsfiberjournal.blogspot.co.uk/2007/03/angora-rabbit-spinning-fiber.html

www.gardengirltv.com/how-to-card-angora-fiber.html

Chapter Six: Breeding Angora Rabbits

The following is intended as a broad overview only.
If you decide to move forward with the breeding of rabbits,
you will need to conduct extensive research in the process
and make sure that you have all the necessary supplies on hands.
Little lives will be depending on you!

B reeding Angora Rabbits can be a wonderful experience but, unless you know the basics, it can be a bit of a challenge. In this chapter you will learn the basics you need to know about how to breed Angora Rabbits on your own.

Included is information about Angora Rabbit breeding habits, age of sexual maturity, litter sizes and more.

1.) Basic Breeding Information

Breeding Angora Rabbits is not necessarily difficult, but there are a few things you should know before you set out to do it. One important piece of information you should know is that Angora Rabbits reach sexual maturity fairly quickly – in many cases, they can become sexually mature by the time they reach 4 to 5 months of age. This information is important for a number of reasons. First, if you plan to raise baby rabbits you will need to separate the sexes before this point to prevent unwanted breeding. Second, you should not attempt to breed an Angora Rabbit before it reaches this age.

Most experienced Angora breeders recommend that you do not breed an Angora until it reaches about 9 months of age. Bucks, or male rabbits, can be bred a little earlier but Does should not be bred before they are 9 months old. You should also be aware that many rabbit breeders state that, if you do plan to breed your Doe, you not wait longer than 1 year to do so. Another important thing to remember is that both Bucks and Does should be groomed and clipped prior to breeding. This is especially important in Does because the rabbit will pull out its own fur to line the nesting box and if the fur is too long, it could strangle the babies.

Experienced Angora breeders will recommend that you always plan your litters – the gestational period of an Angora Rabbit is about 31 days so be sure to mark the day on your calendar. Before breeding, it is important to feed your rabbits a healthy diet so they are in good condition for breeding. If either rabbit is not in optimal condition, it is unlikely to have much interest in breeding – if breeding does occur, it is also less likely to be successful.

2.) The Breeding Process

The breeding process does not require much effort on your part – all you have to do is bring the Doe to the Buck's cage when you determine that the pair is ready for breeding. It is best to bring the Doe to the Buck's cage because the Buck will be less distracted if he is in his own environment. The best time to attempt breeding is in the morning. It is important that you do not leave the rabbits unattended during breeding for several reasons. First, you want to be sure that the act actually takes place. Second, you need to be around to separate the pair if one of the two becomes hostile or aggressive. After coupling the Doe a minimum of three times the Buck should be removed to his cage.

After introducing the pair, breeding should occur fairly quickly. Wait for the Buck to make a high-pitched squeal or grunt and to fall off the Doe – at this point, you should remove the Buck from the cage. How quickly you let them mate again is yet another personal choice. Some breeders advocate three successful mounts during this meeting and no further contact; others give a break of just one hour to ensure a successful mating, while others leave it until the following day to increase the chances of ovulation and a successful pregnancy.

You won't be able to tell for sure that the Doe is pregnant until about 15 days later. Look for swollen nipples at this point and a hardened lower stomach area.

Up until your Doe reaches the halfway point in her pregnancy (about 15 days), continue to feed her normal rations. After this point, however, you should increase her rations by about 50% to provide fuel for milk production. After about 24 days you may be able to feel the babies moving around inside the Doe's belly – if you try to feel them, be very careful so you don't injure the mother or the babies.

About 5 days before your Doe's due date, place a nest box in the cage. Some Does will begin to build a nest before this point but you must still provide a nest box so the babies will be able to stay warm after they are born. Metal nest boxes are preferable to wooden ones because they can be easily disinfected and are less likely to harbor bacteria. Place the nest box in a corner of the cage away from the toilet area where your rabbit can access it easily. If you are using a metal box, remove the bottom and line it with 2 or 3 layers of cardboard then fill the bottom of the box with soft bedding that the Doe can arrange as she likes.

If you are worried about the temperature in your home, you might want to place a specialist low-wattage lamp about 12 inches (30.5 cm) over the box to keep your kits warm. Heat lamps with thermostats are available in a price range of $35 to $50 (£22.75 to £32.50) with replacement bulbs averaging $10 to $15 (£6.50 to £9.75). Ensure that you get a specialist heat lamp to reduce the risk of fire.

3.) Raising the Babies

The average litter size for Angora Rabbits is about 5 to 6 kits. As long as the Doe's first litter is born before she is 1 years old, the birthing process should go smoothly. After this point, the pelvic bones may become fused, making it harder for her to give birth. After the Doe reaches 3 years of age, she should no longer be used for breeding.

Try not to disturb the Doe when she is giving birth, which generally takes place the early morning hours and then wait for her to rest a little bit and to calm down.

After your Doe has kindled – given birth to her young – wait for her to rest a little bit and to calm down. At this point you should carefully remove the nest box from the cage and open it somewhere safe to count the kits. Remove any afterbirth, soiled nesting material and stillborn kits. You should also take a minute to inspect the kits themselves to be sure there are no injuries or birth defects. Place the nesting material and the kits back into the nesting box and place it back in the cage. Be aware that kits sometimes spin in circles in the nest box and this can result in them wrapping the Doe's hair around a paw. If the hair is not removed soon the results can be loss of the limb.

On a daily basis, it is suggested you check the nest to be sure none have died. At this time, the Doe can very protective and although she will know your scent and shouldn't complain, she may jump at you when you probe the nest. I'd recommend you pay her some attention, pet her and perhaps give her a treat to divert her attention before attempting to remove the box to check on the kits. By handling and touching the newborn kits from the start, you will make them gentler and easier to handle.

While the Doe is nursing her young, you should continue to feed her at the increased rate for a few days. After the first few days following the birth, slowly increase the amount of food until the pellets are available at all times. You should always keep fresh hay available in the cage as well. Not only will the Doe eat it but the kits may nibble on it as well as they grow older and their digestive systems begin to develop properly. After 10 to 12 days, the eyes of the kits should begin to open. If they have not opened by day 12, use a damp cotton ball and gently wipe the eyelids from one corner to the other until the eyes open. It is not uncommon for the eyes to close again after opening, so simply repeat the process until the eyes stay open on their own.

By the time the kits reach about 3 to 3 ½ weeks of age they should be ready to live completely outside the nest box. There are conflicting opinions as to whether until that point the kits should be removed from the nest box for cleaning. The general view is that it is best not to disturb the kits as they are born they are virtually hairless so they depend on the nest box and their collective body heat to survive. If you move the baby rabbits from the nest box, they could die from exposure.

However, after several days, the nest box could become smelly and if you can smell urine, most people are of the opinion that you should clean the nest box as quickly as possible, reusing as much of the Doe's fur and other nesting material as you can.

If after you 3 to 3 ½ weeks of age you feel like the babies still need a place to sleep you can place the nesting material in a corner of the cage but remove the box itself. If you are keeping your rabbits outdoors, you may want to clip a specialist low wattage lamp over the nesting area to keep the kits warm enough until they develop enough fur to keep themselves warm.

Once your kits reach 6 to 8 weeks of age, they are ready to be weaned. In many cases, they will naturally wean themselves by nursing less from their mother and accepting more solid food. If you need to wean the kits yourself, however, you can start by removing the largest 2 kits to a separate cage away from the others. After a few days, remove another pair to a separate cage and repeat the process as needed. By the time the kits are about 9 weeks of age you should separate the sexes to prevent unwanted breeding.

Baby rabbits can be free-fed pellets and hay until they reach about 7 months of age. During this period they should be given access to plenty of fresh water. You can begin to introduce small amounts of fresh vegetables (thumb size) once the kits reach 12 weeks of age. As detailed previously, when the kits reach 7 months of age, start to limit them to ½ cup (4 ounces / 115 grams) of pellets per 6 lbs. (2.72 kg) bodyweight. After they reach 1 year of age, you should cut back again to only ¼ to ½ cup (2 to 4 ounces / 57.5 to 115 grams) of pellets a day per 6 lbs. (2.72 kg) bodyweight. At this point, you should also begin to incorporate at least 2 cups (4 to 6 ounces / 113 to 170 grams) of fresh veggies per day in your rabbit's diet.

Chapter Seven: Keeping Healthy

** **Note:** This section may be upsetting to any children who may read it. Sadly like all our pets, Angora Rabbits are susceptible to developing certain health issues.

Although creating the proper diet and habitat are very important, there is more you can do to ensure that your Angora Rabbit remains healthy. You should also familiarize yourself with some of the most common diseases affecting the Angora breed so you can diagnose problems quickly and seek treatment.

In this chapter you will learn how to recognize the common diseases in this breed – you will also learn tips for preventing illness.

Note: Though some health conditions affecting Angora Rabbits can be treated at home, severe cases should always be examined by a veterinarian who will have up to date knowledge and information regarding current treatments for any ailments. If the disease is impacting your rabbit's health or mobility, do not delay in taking it to the vet.

As is true of all pets, the better the care you provide for your Angora, the healthier he will be. Unfortunately, you can't completely prevent your rabbit from ever coming into contact with a disease or getting sick, but you can equip yourself with the knowledge you need to handle the situation. The most common health problems seen include:

- Colibacillosis
- Dental Problems
- Dermatophytosis
- Enterotoxemia
- Fleas/Mites
- Listeriosis
- Mastitis
- Myxomatosis
- Otitis Media

- Papillomatosis
- Pasteurella
- Parasites
- Pneumonia
- Rhinitis
- Sore Hocks
- Uterine Cancer
- Viral Hemorrhagic Disease
- Wool Block

1.) Common Health Problems

Colibacillosis

Colibacillosis is characterized by severe diarrhea and it is often caused by *Escherichia coli*. This disease can be seen in two forms depending on the rabbit's age. Newborn rabbits may exhibit a yellowish diarrhea – in newborns, this condition is often fatal and can affect the entire litter. In weaned rabbits, the intestines may fill with fluid and hemorrhages may surface.

In the case of weaned rabbits, the disease is typically fatal within 2 weeks. If the rabbit survives, it is likely to be stunted. Treatment is not often successful but, in mild cases, antibiotics may help. Rabbits that are severely affected with this disease should be culled to avoid the spread of the disease.

Causes: *Escherichia coli*

Symptoms: yellowish diarrhea in newborns; fluid-filled intestines and hemorrhages in weaned rabbits

Treatment: antibiotics; treatment is not often effective

Dental Problems

All rabbits, including Angora Rabbits, are prone to developing dental problems. The most common issues are overgrown molars and enamel spurs. Your rabbit's teeth may become overgrown or develop spurs if you don't provide enough fiber-rich foods. Fibrous foods are naturally abrasive which helps to keep your rabbit's teeth filed down. In most cases, dental problems require veterinary treatment.

Causes: diet too low in fiber

Symptoms: overgrown molars, enamel spurs

Treatment: veterinary exam and treatment

Dermatophytosis

Also known as ringworm, dermatophytosis caused by either *Trichophyton mentagrophytes* or *Microsporum canis*. These infections typically result from poor husbandry or inadequate nutrition. Ringworm can be transmitted through direct contact with an infected rabbit or sharing tools such as brushes. The symptoms of ringworm include circular raised bumps on the body. The skin is these areas may be red and capped with a white, flaky material. Some

of the most common treatments for ring worm include topical antifungal creams that contain miconazole or itraconazole. A 1% copper sulfate dip may also be effective.

Causes: *Trichophyton mentagrophytes* or *Microsporum canis*; typically results from poor husbandry or inadequate nutrition

Symptoms: circular raised bumps on the body; skin is red and capped with a white, flaky material

Treatment: include topical antifungal creams that contain miconazole or itraconazole; 1% copper sulfate dip

Enterotoxemia

Enterotoxemia is a disease characterized by explosive diarrhea and it typically affects rabbits between the ages of 4 and 8 weeks. Symptoms of this condition include lethargy, loss of condition and greenish-brown fecal matter around the perianal area. In many cases, this condition is fatal within 48 hours.

The primary cause of this disease is *Clostridium spiroforme.*

These organisms are common in rabbits in small numbers but they can become a problem when the rabbit's diet is too low in fiber. Treatment may not be effective due to the rapid progression of the disease but adding cholestryamine or copper sulfate to the diet can help prevent enterotoxemia. Reducing stress in young rabbits and increasing fiber intake can also help.

Causes: *Clostridium spiroforme*

Symptoms: lethargy, loss of condition and greenish-brown fecal matter around the perianal area

Treatment: may not be effective; adding cholestryamine or copper sulfate to the diet can help prevent

Fleas/Mites

Indoor rabbits are unlikely to contract fleas and ticks on their own. If your rabbit spends time outside or if you have other pets that spend time outside however, your rabbit could be at risk. Mites are typically found in the ears and fur of rabbits and they most often present themselves after your rabbit's immune system has already been compromised.

Fur mites tend to stay at the base of the neck or near the rabbit's rear. If left untreated, mites and fleas can cause severe itching, bald spots and bleeding. The best treatment for fleas and mites is a prescription medication called Revolution, known in the UK as Stronghold. Another treatment option in the UK is Ivermectin drops.

Causes: exposure to infested pets, spending time outside

Symptoms: itching, bald spots, bleeding

Treatment: prescription medication; Revolution in the US, known in the UK as Stronghold or Ivermectin drops

Listeriosis

Listeriosis is a type of sporadic septicemia which often causes sudden death or abortion – this condition is most common in pregnant Does. Some of the contributing factors for this disease include poor husbandry and stress. Some of the common symptoms include anorexia, depression and weight loss.

If not properly treated, the *Listeria monocytogenes* responsible for the disease can spread to the blood, liver and uterus. Treatment is not often attempted because diagnosis is not frequently made premortem.

Causes: *Listeria monocytogenes*

Symptoms: anorexia, depression and weight loss; often causes sudden death or abortion

Treatment: not often attempted because diagnosis is not frequently made premortem

Mastitis

This condition is most commonly seen in rabbitries but it can affect single rabbits. Mastitis is a condition that affects pregnant Does and it is caused by *staphylococci* bacteria. The bacteria infect the mammary glands, causing them to become hot, red and swollen. If the disease is allowed to progress, it may cause septicemia and become fatal.

Does affected by mastitis are unlikely to eat but they will crave water. The rabbit may also run a fever. Treatment for this condition may include antibiotic treatment. Penicillin, however, should be avoided because it can cause diarrhea. Kits should not be fostered because they will only end up spreading the disease.

Causes: *staphylococci* bacteria

Symptoms: hot, red and swollen mammary glands; loss of appetite; fever

Treatment: antibiotics

Myxomatosis

Myxomatosis is a viral disease that is caused by *myxoma* virus. This condition is typically fatal and it can be transmitted through direct contact or through biting insects. Some of the initial symptoms of the disease include conjunctivitis, eye discharge, listlessness, anorexia and fever. In severe cases, death may occur after only 48 hours.

Treatment for this condition is generally not effective and it can cause severe and lasting damage. There is however, a vaccine available against myxomatosis. This vaccine should be given after the rabbit reaches 6 weeks of age.

Causes: by *myxoma* virus; transmitted through direct contact or through biting insects

Symptoms: conjunctivitis, eye discharge, listlessness, anorexia and fever

Treatment: generally not effective; vaccine is available

Otitis Media

Also called "wry neck" or "head tilt," otitis media is caused by an infection resulting from *P multocida* or *Encephalitozoon cunuculi*. These bacteria cause the accumulation of fluid or pus in the ear, causing the rabbit to tilt its head. Antibiotic therapy may be effective, though it may just worsen the condition. In most cases, rabbits infected with this condition are culled.

Causes: *P multocida* or *Encephalitozoon cunuculi* bacteria

Symptoms: accumulation of fluid or pus in the ear, causing the rabbit to tilt its head

Treatment: antibiotic therapy may be effective

Papillomatosis

Papillomatosis is fairly common in domestic rabbits and it is caused by the *rabbit oral papillomavirus*. This disease results in the formation of small grey nodules or warts on the underside of the tongue or floor of the mouth. Another type, caused by cottontail papillomavirus, may produce horned warts on the neck, shoulders, ears and abdomen. There is no treatment for these conditions but the lesions typically go away on their own in time.

Causes: *rabbit oral papillomavirus*

Symptoms: small grey nodules or warts on the underside of the tongue or floor of the mouth

Treatment: no treatment; the lesions typically go away on their own in time

Parasites

One of the most common parasites found in rabbits is *Encephalitozoon cuniculi*. This protozoan parasite can survive in the body for years without causing any harm. In some cases, however, the parasite can cause severe damage. This parasite typically causes nerve damage which results in head tilting, incontinence, paralysis and rupture of the lens of the eye.

Intestinal worms are also a common problem in rabbits. Both of these conditions can be treated with de-worming paste. This treatment can be used for infected rabbits and as a preventive against parasites. When used as a preventive, the paste is typically administered twice a year.

Causes: *Encephalitozoon cuniculi,* intestinal worms

Symptoms: head tilting, incontinence, paralysis and rupture of the lens of the eye

Treatment: de-worming paste

Pasteurella

This condition is a respiratory disease caused by the *Pasteurella mulctocida* bacteria which has several strains – some of which have been known to cause pneumonia. Pasteurella is often referred to as "snuffles" because it causes nasal discharge as well as sneezing and congestion. If the rabbit wipes its nose with its paws, the fur on the paws and legs may become matted.

Unfortunately there is no vaccine for pasteurella, though it can often be treated with antibiotics. Depending on the severity of the case, treatment may be continued for weeks or months before symptoms abate. Even if the rabbit's condition improves on antibiotics, the symptoms may return after the treatment is stopped. If the rabbit recovers, it can still become a carrier and spread the disease to others.

Causes: *Pasteurella multocida* bacteria

Symptoms: nasal discharge, sneezing and congestion

Treatment: antibiotic treatment often used, may be necessary to treat for several weeks or months

Pneumonia

Pneumonia is fairly common in domestic rabbits and it is most often a secondary infection. The most common cause of pneumonia in rabbits is *P multocida* bacteria, though other kinds may be involved. A precursor of pneumonia is often upper respiratory disease which may be a result of inadequate ventilation or sanitation.

Some of the common symptoms of pneumonia include listlessness, fever and anorexia. Once they show symptoms, most rabbits succumb to the infection within 1 week. Though antibiotic treatment is often used, it is not typically effective because it may not be administered until the disease is highly advanced.

Causes: *P multocida* bacteria

Symptoms: listlessness, fever and anorexia

Treatment: antibiotic treatment is often used but not typically effective

Rhinitis

Rhinitis is the medical term used to describe sniffling or chronic inflammation in the airway and lungs. This condition is often caused by *Pastuerella*, though *Staphylococcus* or *Streptococcus* may also be involved. The initial symptom of this disease is a thin stream of mucus flowing from the nose. As the disease progresses, the flow may encrust the fur on the paws and chest. Sneezing and coughing may also be exhibited. This condition generally resolves itself but even recovered rabbits can be carriers of the disease.

Causes: is often caused by *Pastuerella*, though *Staphylococcus* or *Streptococcus* may also be involved

Symptoms: sniffling or chronic inflammation in the airway and lungs; thin stream of mucus flowing from the nose

Treatment: generally resolves itself

Uterine Cancer

A common cause of death in female rabbits, uterine cancer can easily be prevented. Spaying female rabbits between the ages of 5 months and 2 years is the best way to prevent this disease. In un-spayed female rabbits, uterine cancer can spread to several different organs before the disease is diagnosed. At that point, treatment is typically ineffective.

Causes: tumor growing in the uterus

Symptoms: other reproductive issues; endometriosis, bulging veins, vaginal discharge, bloody urine

Treatment: spaying female rabbits to prevent; once the cancer develops, treatment is generally ineffective

Viral Hemorrhagic Disease

Also called rabbit hemorrhagic disease, viral hemorrhagic disease is caused by *rabbit calcivirus* and is transmitted through direct contact or contaminated food, water and bedding. Unfortunately, there is no effective treatment for this condition and many rabbits die from it without ever showing symptoms.

Some of the most common symptoms of viral hemorrhagic disease include difficulty breathing, paralysis, lethargy, bloody discharge from the nose, weight loss and convulsions. Once symptoms appear, the disease is typically fatal within 2 weeks.

Causes: *rabbit calcivirus*; transmitted through direct contact or contaminated food, water and bedding

Symptoms: difficulty breathing, paralysis, lethargy, bloody discharge from the nose, weight loss and convulsions

Treatment: no effective treatment; vaccine is available

Wool Block

This breed is especially prone to developing a dangerous condition called Wool Block. This occurs when a ball of hair forms in the stomach and intestines of the rabbit, preventing it from digesting any food. This can lead to inadequate nutrition and eventual starvation and death. Rabbits are incapable of vomiting to clear the hairball.

It is recommended that you speak to your breeder before purchasing your Angora Rabbit as some people feel that a pre-disposition to wool block can be inherited. You can check with your breeder whether it is a problem that they have experienced with their stock. There are several things that you can do to help prevent and diagnose wool block.

Your rabbit must have access to fresh de-chlorinated water at all times and should have lots of exercise. It is essential that Angora Rabbits are fed with a diet that is high in fiber and contains plenty of hay. Many owners supplement with papaya tablets or fresh papaya or pineapple chunks once a week as the enzymes in these help dissolve the food within the fiber and therefore allow it to be passed more easily through the intestines. Other owners will on one day each week feed their rabbit hay and two tablespoons of whole oats and/or extra fresh vegetables. On this day, they do not feed their rabbit any pellets, allowing their stomach an opportunity to clean out.

You should also ensure that your rabbit is groomed properly to reduce the amount of hair that they ingest. Additionally you should study their droppings each day and become familiar with what is normal for your rabbit and note any changes. Droppings that become smaller or are a string of beads mixed with hair, can be a sign of wool block. Changes in eating patterns, weight loss, change in droppings and lethargy can indicate wool block. Due to the seriousness of this condition and the varying opinions on treatment, if you are in any doubt, you should seek veterinarian advice immediately.

2.) Preventing Illness

There are several things you can do to help protect your rabbit against disease. The most important thing is to provide them with a clean, healthy environment. It is essential that you clean your rabbit's cage on a regular basis and provide plenty of fresh water for him to drink. You should also think carefully about their diet and make sure to keep it up to date on vaccinations.

a.) Recommended Vaccinations

Having your rabbit vaccinated is one of the best things you can do to protect it from disease. Two of the most important vaccines for Angora Rabbits are against myxomatosis and viral hemorrhagic disease (VHD) – both of these vaccinations are highly recommended. These vaccines are available as single vaccines, which need to be taken nine days apart every six months, or as a single combined vaccine once a year. In the United States, however, vaccines are generally not required for pet rabbits and many veterinarians do not recommend them unless the rabbit has been exposed to some kind of disease or if you live in a high-risk area and plan to keep your rabbit outdoors.

The best advice is to talk this through with your vet and see what he advises.

It is a good idea to have your rabbit examined as soon as possible by a vet after you bring it home. Your vet will be able to assess your rabbit's condition and set a schedule for future check-ups. Additionally, your vet will also offer recommendations on what vaccines your pet needs and how often he needs them. This will vary from area to area so getting up to date local knowledge is essential. It may seem like a needless cost to take your rabbit to the vet once a year but it can save you a lot of money and heartache in diagnosing serious diseases before they become untreatable.

b.) Dangerous/Toxic Foods

There are certain foods and plants which can be very harmful for your Angora Rabbit. Before you feed your rabbit anything besides Timothy hay or pellets, check the list of foods listed in the Feeding Angora Rabbits section in Chapter Five. You can also check with your vet or local breeder on any local foodstuffs that you might consider feeding your rabbit to avoid heartache.

c.) Ears, Eyes, Nails and Teeth

In addition to vaccinating your rabbit you should also check its condition on your own from time to time. Take a look inside your rabbit's ears for signs of wax buildup or infection – unpleasant odor may also be a sign of infection. Your rabbit's feet should be dry and free from sores. If you notice patches of skin where the fur has worn away or swelling, you should seek immediate veterinary care.

When petting your rabbit, take the time to check its skin and coat. If you notice white flakes or tiny white dots, your rabbit could have mites or fleas.

A rabbit's nails grow continuously so you will need to trim them every six to eight weeks. Trimming your rabbit's nails is not a difficult task but it does require a degree of caution. Inside your rabbit's nail lies the quick – a vein which supplies blood to the nail. If you cut your rabbit's nails too short, you could sever the quick and induce severe bleeding. When clipping your rabbit's nails it is best to only cut off the pointed tip. To be safe, have your veterinarian show you how to properly trim a rabbit's nails before you try it yourself.

If your rabbit's teeth are not properly aligned they can develop a condition called malocclusion. There are three main causes of this, the most common being genetic predisposition, injury or bacterial infection. If you provide your rabbit with adequate chew toys, you shouldn't have to worry about its teeth becoming overgrown. You should, however, make frequent checks to see if the teeth are properly aligned – if they aren't, your rabbit could develop molar spurs or abscesses in the mouth.

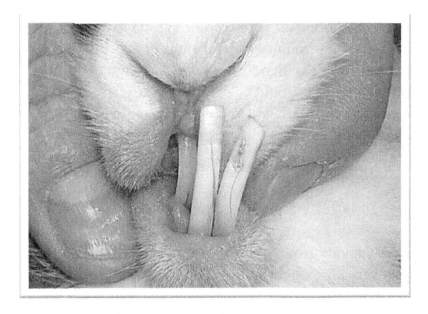

In some rabbits, the teeth are not properly aligned,
a condition called malocclusion.

One of the most common causes of runny eyes in rabbits is a bacterial eye infection. These infections can be very dangerous and must be treated by a veterinarian as soon as possible. In many cases, antibiotics will be prescribed to handle the infection.

Obstructions and inflammation in the eye may be the result of natural or unnatural causes. In some cases, a piece of bedding or some other object may get stuck in the eye causing it to water or become inflamed. It is also possible, however, for a misshapen eyelid or part of the bone in the rabbit's face to cause an obstruction. If the flow of tears is obstructed, they may form a path down the cheek, discoloring the fur. Depending on the cause of the obstruction, surgery may be necessary to correct the issue.

If the rabbit's eyes do not produce enough tears on their own, they may become dry and irritated. When the eyes become too dry, they are more prone to scratches and erosions which can have a devastating effect on your rabbit's ability to see properly. Some of the symptoms of dry eyes include squinting, eye discharge, redness and inflammation. Trauma to the eye can also interfere with the production of tears and should be evaluated by a veterinarian.

Depending what type of litter you use in your rabbit's cage, your rabbit could develop watery eyes as a result of allergies. Dust from the litter, hay or food in your rabbit's cage can get into the eyes and cause irritation. To prevent this from happening, choose litter that is dust-free and make sure the cage is well ventilated.

3.) Pet Insurance

Many pet owners have discovered that pet insurance helps defray the costs of veterinary expenses. Pet insurance is similar to health insurance in that you pay a monthly premium and a deductible (excess in the UK) and the pet insurance pays for whatever is covered in your plan and can include annual exams and blood work. Shopping for pet insurance is similar to shopping for health insurance in the United States.

As with health insurance, the age and the overall health of your rabbit will determine how much you will pay in premiums and deductibles. Ask plenty of questions to determine the best company and plan for your needs. Some of the questions that you should ask are:

- Can you go to your regular vet, or do you have to go to a vet assigned by the pet insurance company?

- What does the insurance plan cover? Does it cover annual exams? Surgeries? Emergency illness and injury?

- Does coverage begin immediately?

- Are pre-existing conditions covered? In addition, if your rabbit develops a health issue and you later have to renew the policy, is that condition covered when you renew your policy?

- Is medication covered?

- Do you have to have pre-authorization before your pet receives treatment? What happens if your rabbit has the treatment without pre-authorization?

- Is there a lifetime maximum benefit amount? If so, how much is that amount?

Take the time to research your pet insurance options. Compare the different plans available, what each covers, and the cost before making the decision on which is best for you and your pet. Pet insurance may not be the answer for everyone and while it may not be a feasible option for you, consider having a backup plan, just in case your rabbit requires emergency care or you run into unexpected veterinarian costs.

A simple way to prepare for an emergency is to start a veterinary fund for your rabbit. Decide to put a certain amount of money aside each week, each month, or each paycheck to use in the case of an emergency. Think about the potential financial costs of veterinary care and plan for how you will pay for it now instead of waiting until something occurs.

Companies in the United States offering pet insurance:

Healthy Paws
HealthyPawsPetInsurance.com

PetPlan
GoPetPlan.com

Embrace
EmbracePetInsurance.com

Trupanion
Trupanion.com

Pets Best
PetsBest.com

Pet Premium
Enroll.PetPremium.com

The ASPCA
ASPCAPetInsurance.com

PetInsurance
PetInsurance.com

Pet First
PetFirst.com

24PetWatch
24PetWatch.com

Pet insurance companies in the United Kingdom include:

DirectLine
Directline.com/pet-insurance

VetsMediCover
Vetsmedicover.co.uk

PetPlan
Petplan.co.uk

Churchill
Churchill.com/pet-insurance

Animal Friends
Animalfriends.org.uk

Healthy Pets
Healthy-pets.co.uk

For a comprehensive comparison of policies see:
Money.co.uk/pet-insurance.htm

Please note that all companies and links were valid at the time of publication in early 2014, but like all Internet content are subject to change. Since pet insurance is growing rapidly in popularity, use the search engine of your choice to look for additional coverage options. Note that the vast majority of sites allow visitors to obtain an estimate price quote online.

Chapter Eight: Showing Angora Rabbits

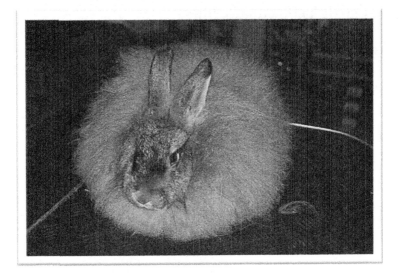

Showing rabbits can be a very thrilling and challenging experience. It is not something you should set out to do without careful consideration, however. All rabbits are judged according to a very strict breed standard and if your rabbit does not meet that standard, it will not do well in the competition.

In this chapter you will learn about the Angora Rabbit breed standard as well as other tips for success at rabbit shows.

1.) Breed Standard

The breed standard of the Angora Rabbit is the standard to which all Angora Rabbits are compared in show. Judges are given a summary of points and evaluate each individual rabbit in the proper categories. Point totals are awarded out of 100 points possible.

a.) UK Angora Breed Standard

In the UK, the only acceptable breed standard for Angora Rabbits is that of the English Angora. The breed standard in the UK is as follows:

Wool Quality: (30 possible points)

Wool Quantity and Length: (25 possible points)

Front: (10 possible points)

Head and Ears: (10 possible points)

Size and Shape: (10 possible points)

Feet: (5 possible points)

Condition: (10 possible points)

Total Points Possible = 100 points

In-Depth Explanation of Points:

Wool Quality: The ideal wool quality for the Angora rabbit is silky and lustrous. The easiest coat to maintain good quality with is a dense coat that is not too fine – this will prevent matting and make grooming easier.

Wool Quantity and Length: Angora Rabbits are generally thought to be in their prime for showing between 5 and 7 months of age. At this time, their wool is typically about 5 to 7 inches (13 to 18 cm) long. According to the breed standard, the wool should be even and full all over the body, clear to the skin.

Front: The front of the rabbit should be full and prominent on the chest and the sides of the neck. Ideally, the face should be clean and almost burrowed in a pillow of fur. The chest and shoulders should be prominent and the head well off the ground.

Head and Ears: The ideal Angora Rabbit will have a broad and short head with short, well-wooled and tufted ears. The head should be mildly broad across the nostrils to create a flat and vertical profile. When viewed from the front, the head should look almost rectangular with a fringe of fur on top.

Size and Shape: In terms of size and shape, Angora Rabbits should be round and well-furred. At 5 months, the rabbit should weigh around 5.5 lbs. (2.49 kg) but not more than 7.5 lbs. (3.4 kg). As for shape, the rabbit should resemble a snowball with a short, cobby body (round with very small neck) and a dramatic rise over the hind quarters.

Feet: The feet should be well furnished and covered with long thick wool.

Condition: The rabbit should be clean, well-nourished and properly groomed for show.

b.) ARBA English Angora Breed Standard

Show Classifications: White and Colored

General Type: (33 points possible)

> *Body:* (15 possible points)
>
> *Head:* (5 possible points)
>
> *Ears:* (5 possible points)
>
> *Eyes:* (2 possible points)
>
> *Feet and Legs:* (5 possible points)
>
> *Tail:* (1 possible point)

Wool: (57 points possible)

> *Density:* (25 possible points)
>
> *Texture:* (20 possible points)
>
> *Length:* (12 possible points)

Color: (5 points possible)

Condition: (5 points possible)

Total Points = 100 points possible

In-Depth Explanation of Points:

General Type

Body: The body of an Angora Rabbit should be short and compact, having a full chest and rounded shoulders. The hips should be wide, tapering slightly to the shoulders which are of good depth. The top line should rise to the highest point over the hips, rounding down to the base of the tail. When posed correctly, the rabbit should look like a snowball.

Head: The head should be short and broad in order to balance with the body. It should be close-set with the body, having dense bangs and trimmings on the sides. The head should be flat across the nostrils.

Ears: The rabbit's ears should be relatively short and carried in a close "V" shape. The ears should balance with the body, having abundant fringe and tassels.

Eyes: The eyes should be bold and bright.

Feet and Legs: The legs should be medium-boned and in good proportion to the body. Legs should be well-covered in wool and free from mats – back legs should have a thick fringe of wool. Toenails on colored rabbits should be colored and white on white rabbits.

Tail: The tail should be straight and well-covered in wool. It should be proportional to the body in size.

Wool

Density: The greatest density possible is preferred in Angora wool. The density should be even all around the body, including the back and belly. To determine the density, judges will feel the body, side, rump and chest. Matting or felted wool should not be mistaken for density.

Texture: The texture of the wool should be silky and healthy – it should not have a flat appearance by parting over the back. The guard hairs should be evident in the under wool which should be crimped.

Length: The length of the wool should be even over the whole body, though blending in length from the back and sides to the belly is acceptable. The ideal wool length is between 3.5 and 5 inches (8.89 to 12.7 cm) and coats over 5 inches (12.7 cm) long are not to be given an advantage.

Color

Matches description in the list of Angora colors recognized by the ARBA. These include: ruby-eyed white, pointed white, self, shaded, agouti and broken.

Agouti (A), Black (B) and Solid/Self (C) are dominant genes in Angora rabbits. There are also genes for the density of color -- D is full density and d is dilute. In terms of show, judges tend to prefer rabbits with more intense color (D), so it if you plan to show your rabbits you should favor rabbits with genetics D over d. You may also want to avoid breeding tortoiseshell rabbits to solid color Angoras because the tortoiseshell genes may dilute the solid coloration.

Condition

The rabbit should appear to be in good health, having a good coat. The flesh should be firm without too much fat or too little, creating a bony effect.

2.) What to Know Before Showing

There are a number of things you should know before attempting to show your Angora Rabbit. The first thing you need to do is to familiarize yourself with the breed standard and to make sure your own rabbit(s) meet the standard.

In addition to the breakdown of points, you should keep in mind the faults and disqualifications for the breed.

Faults/Disqualifications for Angora Rabbits:

- Narrow or wedge-shaped head

- Long plain ears

- Plain (unfurnished) feet

- Matted coat

- Coarse texture in coat

- Bad condition

- Lopped ears

- Silvered ears and nose (in smokes and blues)

- Putty nose

- White toenails (in colored rabbits)

- White patches on body (in colored rabbits except under the tail in agouti)

You should also be aware that the British Rabbit Council (BRC) judge colored Angoras on a slightly different standard of points than white Angoras. The only difference is that 5 points are deducted from the Quality and Quantity of Wool categories and allocated to a new category, Solid Color.

The colors recognized by the BRC include:

Golden	Chocolate
Sooty Fawn	Smoke
Cream	Blue
Blue-Cream	Brown-Grey (Agouti)
Sable – Light, Medium, Dark	Blue-Grey (Agouti)
	Chinchilla (Agouti)
Marten – Light, Medium, Dark	Cinnamon (Agouti)

Note: All Angora Rabbits have a multi-layered coat and the tips of each layer are darker than the layer beneath. This produces banding in all colored Angoras. Colors Angoras should not be penalized for light bands in the top color, but uniform color is preferred.

3.) Things to Bring to a Rabbit Show

The key to success in rabbit shows is to be prepared. This involves making sure your rabbit meets the breed standard and arranging the rabbit properly for judging. You should also prepare yourself by bringing along an emergency kit, just in case.

Included in your emergency kit should be:

- Nail clippers – for emergency nail trimming
- Antibiotic ointment
- Band-Aids – for minor injuries to self, not rabbit
- Hydrogen peroxide – for cleaning injuries and spots on white coats
- Slicker brush – to smooth rough coats
- Black felt-tip pen
- Business cards
- Paper towels – because you never know
- Scrap carpet square – for last-minute grooming
- Collapsible stool – when chairs are not available
- Extra clothes
- Supplies for your rabbits

Chapter Nine: Angora Rabbit Care Sheet

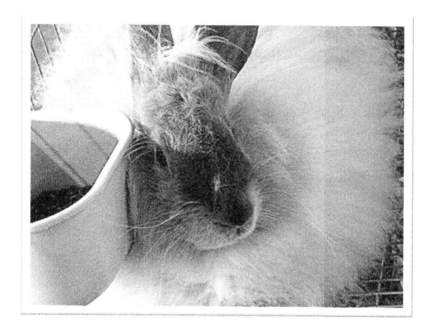

In this chapter you will find summaries of all the Angora Rabbit facts that we have discussed. Included in these summaries is valuable information about the breed itself as well as cage requirements, nutritional needs and breeding information.

It sometimes helps to have everything simplified in one place to refresh your memory and have it as a handy reference point. I've also included some ideas in case of the unexpected happening to you.

1.) Basic Information

Scientific Name: *Oryctolagus cuniculus*

Classification: wool breed

Weight: varies by breed 4.5 to 12 lbs. plus (2.04 to 5.44 kg)

Body Shape: rounded with full chest and shoulders

Body Structure: short and compact, looks like a fluffy snowball

Ears: erect, held close in a "V" shape

Eyes: to match coat color

Coat: soft and silky; 5 to 7 inches (12.7 to 17.8 cm) long; multi-layered

Coat Color: ruby-eyed white, pointed white, self, shaded, agouti, broken, smoke, blue, golden, chocolate and lilac

Diet: herbivorous

Foods: commercial rabbit pellets, Timothy hay, vegetables and fruits

Supplements: generally not required if the diet is sufficient in fiber and protein

Lifespan: average 7 to 12 years

2.) Cage Set-up Guide

Of course, the type of Angora Breed you get has some impact on the minimum size but the figures quoted are just a guide. I recommend the biggest you can comfortably have at all times.

Minimum Cage Size: 30 x 30 inches (76.2 x 76.2 cm)

Minimum Cage Height: 18 inches (45.7 cm)

Location Options: indoor or outdoor

Indoor Location Tips: away from drafts, not in direct sunlight, away from heating/cooling vents

Outdoor Location Tips: ensure that your rabbit is not too cold or too hot, provide shade and ensure that cage/pen sure from predators

Cage Types: single-level, multi-level, open pen

Cage Materials: galvanized welded wire, solid metal or plastic bottom

Bedding: non-toxic pellets, fresh hay, newspaper

Accessories: water bottle, food bowls, hay wheel, litter pan, chew toys, shelter

3.) Nutrition and Feeding Facts

Diet Basics: about 18% protein, high fiber

Main Diet: high-quality grass hay (Timothy hay, orchard hay, Bermuda grass)

Commercial Pellets: about 18% protein

Supplemental Foods: fresh vegetable greens, fruits, seeds

Amount to Feed (juvenile): unlimited hay, unlimited pellets

Amount to Feed (adult): unlimited hay; ¼ to ½ cup (2 to 4 ounces / 57.5 to 115 grams) of pellets a day per 6 lbs. (2.72 kg) bodyweight; 2 cups (4 to 6 ounces / 113 to 170 grams) of fresh green vegetables daily

Other Needs: unlimited supply of fresh water

Treats: fresh fruit, carrots, sunflower seeds, rolled oats, dried bread

4.) Breeding and Rearing Facts

Sexual Maturity: 4 to 5 months of age

Breeding Age: at least 9 months to 1 year

Gestation Period: about 31 days

Signs of Pregnancy: swollen nipples and hardened belly (15 days)

Pregnant Diet: normal rations to day 15, then increase by 50% daily ration

Nest Box Materials: metal box is ideal, line bottom with cardboard and hay

Nest Box Dimensions: 10 x 20 x 10 inches (25.4 x 50.8 x 25.4 cm)

Insert Nest Box: about 5 days before due date

Average Litter Size: 5 to 6 kits

Eyes Open: 10 to 12 days after birth

Leave Nest Box: 3 to 3 ½ weeks

Weaning Age: 6 to 8 weeks

Separate Sexes: 9 weeks

5.) Planning for the Unexpected

If something happens to you, you want to know that your rabbit and any other pets will be properly cared for and loved. Some cell phones allow you to input an ICE (In Case of Emergency) number with notes. If your cell phone has such an option, use it. If it does not, write the following information on a piece of a paper and put it in your wallet with your driver's license:

- The names of each of your pets, including your rabbit.

- The names and phone numbers of family members or friends who have agreed to temporarily care for your pets in an emergency.

- The name and phone number of your veterinarian.

Be sure to also talk with your neighbors, letting them know how many pets you have and the type of pets. That way, if something happens to you, they can alert the authorities, ensuring your pets do not linger for days before they are found.

If you fail to do that and something happens to you, someone will find your rabbit and any other pets and will need to know what to do to ensure that they are cared for. It is a good idea in the case of an emergency, to ask several friends or family members to be responsible for taking care of your pets should something happen to you. Prepare instructions for the intended guardians, providing amended instructions as necessary. Also, be sure to provide each individual with a key to your home (remember to inform your home insurance company so that this does not affect your coverage).

Instructions should include:

- The name and phone numbers of each individual who agreed to take care of your rabbit and other pets.

- Your pet's diet and feeding schedule.

- The name and phone number of your veterinarian.

- Any health problems and medications your rabbit may take on a daily basis, including dosage instructions, instructions on how to give the medicine, and where the medicine is kept.

Put as much information as necessary to ensure the guardians can provide the same level of care to which your rabbit is accustomed.

Chapter Ten: General Care Questions

After reading through this book, I hope you will feel better prepared to look after your Angora Rabbit. In case you still have a few general questions about keeping rabbits, this chapter may be able to help.

Here, you will find the answers to several common questions regarding keeping and caring for rabbits including breeding, spaying/neutering, buying or adopting a rabbit and veterinary care.

Q: What are the health benefits of spaying/neutering?

A: Some rabbits exhibit behavioral changes if they are not spayed or neutered. They may become more aggressive and they may spray urine. For female rabbits, spaying greatly reduces the risk for uterine cancer. Uterine cancer is one of the most common causes of death in un-spayed rabbits and it is often untreatable by the time a diagnosis is made. Neutering male rabbits will help prevent them from fighting with other rabbits which could also serve to extend their lives.

Q: What precautions should I take when buying from a breeder?

A: You should take the same precautions in buying from a breeder as you would in a pet store or shelter. You will need to examine the individual rabbits to make sure they are healthy before you even begin to talk about purchasing one. In addition to checking the health of the stock, you should also determine the breeder's experience and credentials. Ask the breeder questions to determine how much they know about the breed how much experience they have and whether or not they have the required license or registration to breed rabbits legally. It is always a good idea to tour their facilities to check the standards kept.

Q: Can I build my own rabbit cage?

A: Yes, you can build your own rabbit cage as long as you use the appropriate materials and make it the right size. The easiest way to make your own rabbit cage is to use stackable wire cubes to create a multi-level cage. Insert wooden dowels through the gaps to create supports for wooden shelves and line the shelves with towels to make them more comfortable for your rabbit. Make sure that any sharp ends are filed down and covered with cloth to prevent injury to yourself and your rabbit.

Q: What are the benefits of adopting an adult rabbit?

A: Many people prefer to buy baby rabbits because they want to raise the rabbit themselves. While this is a wonderful experience, there are also several unique benefits involved in adopting an adult rabbit. Adult rabbits are more likely to already be litter trained which will save you the hassle of having to do it yourself. It is also more likely that the rabbit will already be spayed or neutered because this is a policy most shelters enforce. Adopting an adult rabbit may also be a little cheaper than buying a baby rabbit from a pet store or breeder.

Q: Can I let my rabbit play outside?

A: Yes, you can let your rabbit play outside as long as you take a few precautions. First, it is important that your rabbit receives all the necessary vaccinations to keep him protected against disease. Second, you should build or buy an outdoor rabbit run that will keep your rabbit safe while he is outside. Even while your rabbit is confined to the run you should keep an eye on him.

Q: How often should I clean my rabbit's cage?

A: The best answer to this question is "as often as necessary". If you have multiple rabbits in one cage or one messy rabbit, you may need to clean out the cage more often than you would for a single rabbit. Generally, you should plan to change your rabbit's bedding once a week but you may need to clean the litter box two or three times within that same period of time.

Q: What vaccinations are required for rabbit?

A: Vaccinations are not required but certain ones are highly recommended. The two most important vaccines for rabbits are against myxomatosis and viral hemorrhagic disease (VHD). Both of these diseases are very serious and often fatal. Aside from preventive vaccination, treatments for these diseases are typically ineffective.

It is also often required for getting pet insurance, holiday boarding and attending events. After reading the health section of this book you should know that many rabbit diseases progress rapidly, often without showing any symptoms. This being the case, taking your rabbit to the vet once or twice a year may be the only way to catch diseases before they progress beyond repair.

Q: Do I need to have my rabbit examined by a vet?

A: Again, it is your choice whether or not you provide your rabbit with routine veterinary care. Some rabbit owners prefer to save themselves the expense of veterinary visits while others see the value in it. The benefit of taking your rabbit in for regular check-ups is that you can catch diseases and conditions in the early stages and provide treatment. You can also keep your rabbit up to date on recommended vaccinations

Chapter Eleven: Relevant Websites

Whan you start looking around the internet it can take some time to track down exactly what you are looking for.

Shopping

A one-stop shop for all your rabbit needs is what is required and the sites below offer you the convenience of pulling together many of the best products from around the web. Enjoy Shopping!

United States of America www.rabbitsorbunnies.com

United Kingdom www.rabbitsorbunnies.co.uk

The following websites will have information for both U.K. and U.S.A. residents in the following categories:

- Food for Angora Rabbits

- Care for Angora Rabbits

- Health Information for Angora Rabbits

- General Information for Angora Rabbits

- Showing Angora Rabbits

1.) Food for Angora Rabbits

These websites will provide you with the information that you need to know about feeding your Angora Rabbits a healthy diet. You will receive information about your rabbit's nutritional needs, food options and more.

United States of America Websites:

"Feeding the Angora Rabbit & Wool Block Prevention." Avillion Farm.
http://avillionfarm.com/pdflib/RabbitFeedAndWB.pdf

"Angora Rabbits 101: Feeding Angora Rabbits Organically." Joybilee Farm.
http://joybileefarm.com/angora-rabbits-101-feeding-angora-rabbits-organically/

United Kingdom Websites:

Jennings, Pat. "Hints on Herbs." National Angora Rabbit Club of Great Britain,
http://nationalangoraclub.webs.com/Hints%20on%20Herbs%20(Pat%20Jennings)%20NAC%201991.pdf

"Rabbit – Facts and Care Sheet." Freshfields Animal Rescue.
www.freshfieldsrescue.org.uk/images/uploads/articles/Rabbit_care_sheet1.pdf

"Feeding Your Rabbit." Croft Veterinary Surgeons.
www.croftvets.co.uk/rabbits/feeding-your-rabbit

2.) Care for Angora Rabbits

The websites in this section will provide you with a wealth of information that you need to know about when caring for Angora Rabbits. You will find information regarding housing and raising rabbits as well as tips for purchasing a rabbit from a breeder.

United States of America Websites:

"New Owner Guide," Appalachian Angora Rabbit Club, www.appalachianangoras.org/new-owner-guide.html

"Angora Rabbit Care Guidelines," International Association of German Angora Rabbit Breeders, www.iagarb.com/angoracare.html

Glenn, Pat. "Tips for Grooming Angoras." National Angora Rabbit Breeders Club. www.nationalangorarabbitbreeders.com/tipsforgrooming.pdf

"Angora Care." Tenney's Rabbitry. www.theangorarabbit.com/catalog.php?category=7

United Kingdom Websites:

"Keeping Your Rabbit Happy." CottonTails Rescue, www.cottontails-rescue.org.uk/rabbits.asp

"Rabbits." The Royal Society for the Prevention of Cruelty to Animals. www.rspca.org.uk/allaboutanimals/pets/rabbits

"Angora Rabbit Online Technical Manual."
AngoraRabbit.com.
https://angorarabbit.com/hutch/articles.php?cat_id=4

3.) Health Information for Angora Rabbits

The websites in this section will provide you with a lot of
the information you need to know about to help keep your
Angora Rabbits healthy. You will find information about
common health problems, vaccinations and other health-
related information.

United States of America Websites:

Bartold, Margaret. "Enteritis." National Angora Rabbit
Breeders Club.
www.nationalangorarabbitbreeders.com/enteritis-
article.pdf

"Rabbit Health – With Proper Care Rabbits Make Charming
Companions." RabbitMatters.com.
www.rabbitmatters.com/rabbitcare.html

"Parasitic Diseases of Rabbits." The Merck Veterinary
Manual.
www.merckmanuals.com/vet/exotic_and_laboratory_anim
als/rabbits/parasitic_diseases_of_rabbits.html

United Kingdom Websites:

"Hand-Rearing Orphan Baby Rabbits," CottonTails Rescue.
www.cottontails-rescue.org.uk/handrear.asp

"Health." The People's Dispensary for Sick Animals.
www.pdsa.org.uk/pet-health-advice/rabbits/health

"Rabbits." The Royal Society for the Prevention of Cruelty to Animals.
www.rspca.org.uk/allaboutanimals/pets/rabbits

4.) General Information for Angora Rabbits

The following websites will provide you with general information about Angora Rabbits – here you will find information regarding the history of the Angora Rabbit breed, general facts and owner testimonials.

United States of America Websites:

Samson, Leslie. "The German Angora." International Association of German Angora Rabbit Breeders,
www.iagarb.com/germangiant.html

Lewis, Dave. "The Joys of Angora Rabbits." National Angora Rabbit Breeders Club.
www.nationalangorarabbitbreeders.com/joysofangoras.pdf

"Angora Rabbits." Animal-World Encyclopedia.
http://animal-world.com/encyclo/critters/rabbits/angora.php

United Kingdom Websites:

"Rabbit – Angora Breed Profile." PetPlanet.co.uk.
www.petplanet.co.uk/small_breed_profile.asp?sbid=8

Varga, Victoria. "Angora Rabbits: The Wool Industry's Pride and Joy." Homestead.org, http://homestead.org/VictoriaVarga/AngoraRabbits/FuzzyBunny.htm

Osborn, Phill and Judy. "Keeping Angora Rabbits for Fiber." Pocket Farm Magazine. www.pocketfarm.co.uk/keeping-angora-rabbits-for-fibre/

5.) Showing Angora Rabbits

The following websites will provide you with information about showing Angora Rabbits in either the U.S.A. or the U.K. You will find information regarding the breed standard, how points are awarded and how to prepare for shows.

United States of America Websites:

"AARC Specialty Shows," Appalachian Angora Rabbit Club, www.appalachianangoras.org/aarc-specialty-shows.html

"Events of Interest," Southern Angora Rabbit Club, http://southernangorarc.weebly.com/events-of-interest.html

"Standard of the German Angora," International Association of German Angora Rabbit Breeders, www.iagarb.com/standards.html

United Kingdom Websites:

"Breed Standard," National Angora Rabbit Club of Great Britain,
http://nationalangoraclub.webs.com/breed-standard

"Showing Your Rabbits." Huddersfield & District Fanciers Society.
www.huddersfieldrabbits.org.uk/showingrabbits.htm

Hobbs-Fothergrill, Mrs. Yvonne. "Exhibition Grooming." National Angora Rabbit Club of Great Britain.
http://nationalangoraclub.webs.com/exhibition%20groomin g%20(yvonne).pdf

Index

A

AARC 13, 128
accessories..29, 30, 31, 34, 52, 54, 112
alfalfa hay 55
American Rabbit Breeders' Association... 5, 10
animal movement license.. 25
antibiotics 81, 88, 96
ARBA 5, 10, 15, 16, 17, 18, 40, 41, 104, 106

B

baby rabbits.. 3, 40, 72, 77, 78, 119
bacteria... 74, 85, 86, 88, 89
bedding.................................... 29, 30, 32, 33, 34, 48, 53, 74, 91, 96, 112, 120
Bermuda grass 56, 113
Beveren Club 11
birth 75
breed standard/s 6, 10, 101, 102, 103, 104, 107, 109, 128
breeder/breeders 39, 41, 44, 45
breeders 11, 12, 13, 17, 25, 29, 38, 40, 41, 42, 44, 72, 118, 119, 125
breeding 4, 2, 3, 11, 24, 45, 71, 72, 73, 75, 78, 110, 117, 144
British Fur Rabbit Society... 11
British Rabbit Council 11, 42
Buck 2, 3, 72, 73

C

cage .. 28, 29, 30, 31, 32, 33, 34, 35, 36, 47, 48, 49, 50, 51, 52, 53, 54, 66, 73, 74, 75, 76,
    77, 92, 96, 110, 112, 118, 120
chew toys..8, 29, 30, 33, 52, 54, 95, 112
clean up 36, 61
cleaning 31, 34, 77, 109
clipping 94
Colibacillosis 81
commercial pellets 32, 55, 58, 59, 113
common diseases 79

competition 101
costs.. 29, 30, 31, 33

D

death 84, 85, 86, 90, 118
Dental Problems 81, 82
Dermatophytosis 82
diarrhea 81, 83, 85
diet 53, 55, 58, 59, 60, 78, 79, 82, 83, 93, 111, 113, 115
disease................. 25, 45, 81, 83, 84, 85, 86, 87, 89, 90, 92, 93, 119, 121
disease/diseases 80, 88
Doe/Does..2, 72, 73, 74, 75, 76, 77, 84, 85

E

ears.......................1, 2, 3, 6, 16, 17, 27, 35, 45, 83, 87, 94, 102, 103, 105, 107, 111
English Angora 5, 7, 10, 15, 17, 18, 26, 41, 102, 104
Enterotoxemia 83
exercise..50
exercise pen..34, 49

F

facts 4, 2, 4, 6, 7, 8, 110, 112, 113, 127
feed 32, 55, 56, 59, 60, 72, 74, 76, 94, 113
feeding.................................. 2, 23, 55, 58, 59, 60, 94, 112, 115, 124
fiber 55, 81, 82, 83, 111, 112
fleas 51, 83, 84, 94
food 18, 29, 32, 34, 55, 56, 59, 60, 76, 77, 81, 90, 91, 94, 96, 111, 113, 123, 124
food bowl/dishes... 29, 30, 34, 52, 112
food/foods..53
French Angora 5, 7, 10, 15, 18, 26, 40, 144
fresh fruits 55
fur 1, 7, 9, 16, 17, 27, 36, 47, 51, 55, 62, 63, 64, 72, 77, 83, 84, 89, 94, 96, 103

G

German Angora 5, 7, 12, 15, 16, 17, 40, 65, 125, 127, 128, 144
gestational period..72
Giant Angora..5, 7, 10, 15, 17, 18, 26, 40
grooming 15, 28, 31, 36, 63, 65, 70, 103, 109
grooming supplies 31

H

habitat 29, 46, 47, 79
hay 32, 48, 53, 55, 56, 58, 59, 61, 76, 78, 112, 113, 114
hay wheel 52, 53, 56, 112
head tilt 86, 87, 88
health 23, 27, 34, 35, 43, 45, 46, 61, 79, 81, 107, 117, 118, 120, 123, 126
health problems 43, 80, 116
healthy 43, 44, 45, 47, 55, 58, 60, 79, 92, 106, 118, 126
healthy diet 46, 55, 72, 124
history 4, 5, 9, 10, 11, 45, 127
household pets 2, 5, 35
housing 23, 125
human health considerations 37
hutch 32, 52

I

independent breeder 39
indoors versus outdoors 48
infection 82, 86, 89, 94, 95, 96
initial costs 29, 31, 32
intestinal worms 87, 88

K

kindling 3
kits 3, 44, 74, 75, 76, 77, 78, 85, 114

L

length 6, 102, 103, 106
license 24, 25, 114, 118
licensing requirements 23, 25
Listeriosis 84
litter 3, 31, 32, 36, 40, 44, 48, 52, 61, 62, 71, 72, 75, 81, 96, 112, 114, 119, 120
litter box 61, 62

M

Mastitis 85
mites 83, 84, 94

monthly costs 23, 29, 32, 33, 34
Myxomatosis 85, 86, 93, 120

N

nails 35, 94, 95
National Angora Club of Great Britain 12, 42
National Angora Rabbit Breeders Club 10, 12, 41, 125, 126, 127, 144, 145
National Rabbit Council of Great Britain 11
nest box 74, 75, 77, 114
nursing 3, 76, 77
nutritional needs 55, 110, 124

O

odor 36, 51, 60, 94
orchard hay 113
oryctolagus cocincinus 111
other pets 5, 23, 27, 83, 114, 115
Otitis Media 86

P

Papillomatosis 87
parasites 51, 87, 88
pellet/pellets 53
pellets 56, 58, 60, 76, 78, 94, 112, 113
permit 24, 25
personalities 8, 27
pet insurance 33, 97, 98, 99, 100
pet store 24, 29, 38, 39, 41, 49, 50, 118, 119
pets 2, 4, 5, 9, 24, 27, 34, 79, 84, 114, 115
pneumonia 89
Pneumonia 88, 89
pregnant 73, 84, 85, 113
pros and cons 23, 29, 35, 51
protein 55, 58, 111, 112, 113

R

rabbit breeds 10, 11, 23, 29, 39
rabbit clubs 11
rabbit food 32

rabbit hemorrhagic disease 90
rabbit pellets 58, 111
rabbit rescue group. 39
rabbit run.. 49, 51, 119
rabbit shows 10, 11, 101, 109
Rhinitis.. 89
ringworm 82

S

Satin Angora 5, 7, 10, 15, 18, 40
sexual maturity.. 71, 72, 113
shelter... 47, 53, 112, 118, 119
shopping 39, 97, 122
showing 6, 11, 91, 101, 103, 107, 123, 128
size.. 7, 16, 18, 28, 30, 47, 75, 78, 102, 103, 105, 112, 114, 118
Southern Angora Rabbit Club 13, 128
spayed or neutered 24, 29, 90, 117, 118, 119
stress 83, 84
symptoms 81, 82, 83, 84, 85, 86, 87, 88, 89, 90, 91, 96, 120

T

teeth 35, 45, 54, 81, 82, 94, 95
temperature 51, 74
Timothy hay.. 55, 56, 94, 111, 113
toys 29, 32, 54
travel carrier 30, 53
treats 55, 59, 60, 113

U

United Angora Rabbit Club 12, 13
uterine cancer 90, 118

V

vaccinations 29, 30, 40, 93, 119, 120, 121, 126
vegetables 32, 55, 58, 59, 78, 111, 113
vet120
vet/veterinarian...............29, 30, 33, 40, 41, 52, 56, 60, 80, 93, 94, 96, 97, 98, 115, 120
veterinary care 30, 32, 33, 94, 98, 117, 120
viral hemorrhagic disease 90, 91, 93, 120

W

water 34, 52, 53, 55, 61, 78, 85, 90, 91, 92, 96, 113

water bottle 30, 34, 52, 53, 112

weaned 58, 77, 81

weight 7, 8, 17, 84, 85, 91, 111

wire cages 49

wool 1, 4, 5, 6, 7, 8, 9, 13, 17, 18, 26, 27, 34, 35, 36, 55, 62, 65, 102, 103, 104, 105, 106, 111

wool block 91

wry neck 86

Photo Credits

Cover Design:- Liliana Gonzalez Garcia, ipublicidades.com (info@ipublicidades.com)

Title Page Photo by Lanafactum
http://commons.wikimedia.org/wiki/File:White_Satin_Angora_Rabbit.jpg

Photo by Flickr user Jigra Knits
www.flickr.com/photos/jigraknits/231095499/sizes/z/in/photostream/

Photo by Mghamburg via Wikimedia Commons
http://commons.wikimedia.org/wiki/File:EnglishAngoraRabbit.jpg

Photo by Flickr user YoAmes
www.flickr.com/photos/24013072@N05/4023465001/sizes/z/in/photostream/

Photo by Flickr user distar97
www.flickr.com/photos/dennisharper/5799133348/

Photo by Clevername
http://commons.wikimedia.org/wiki/File%3AEnglishangora.jpg

Photo by Flickr user YoAmes
www.flickr.com/photos/24013072@N05/4024150648/sizes/z/in/photostream/

Photo by Garitzko
http://commons.wikimedia.org/wiki/File:Angorakaninchen.jpg

Photo by Flickr user YoAmes
www.flickr.com/photos/24013072@N05/4024148200/sizes/z/in/photostream/

Photo by Flickr user Distar97
www.flickr.com/photos/dennisharper/7155120231/sizes/c/in/photostream

Photo by Oldhaus
http://commons.wikimedia.org/wiki/File:Joey_Giant_Angora_Buck.jpg

Photo by Verolg
http://commons.wikimedia.org/wiki/File:Conejo_angora.jpg

Photo by Verolg
http://commons.wikimedia.org/wiki/File:Conejo_de_angora.jpg

Photo by Ross Little via Wikimedia Commons
https://en.m.wikipedia.org/wiki/File:Fluffy_white_bunny_rabbit.jpg

Photo by Flickr user Distar97
www.flickr.com/photos/dennisharper/7155120527/sizes/z/in/photostream/

Photo by Clevername

http://en.m.wikipedia.org/wiki/File:Satinangora.jpg

Photo by Loggie-log

http://commons.wikimedia.org/wiki/File:FrenchAngora.jpg

Photo by Verolg

http://commons.wikimedia.org/wiki/File:Conejo_angora1.jpg

Photo by Flickr user YoAmes

www.flickr.com/photos/24013072@N05/4024047210/sizes/z/in/photostream/

Photo Purchased from BigStockPhoto.net

Photo by Flickr user Jigra Knits
www.flickr.com/photos/jigraknits/231095501/sizes/z/in/photostre
am/

Photo by Uwe Gille
http://commons.wikimedia.org/wiki/File:Bradygnathia-superior-
rabbit.jpg

Photo by Radosław Drożdżewski (Zwiadowca21)
http://commons.wikimedia.org/wiki/File:Angorakaninchen_002.J
PG

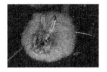

Photo by Lanafactum
http://commons.wikimedia.org/wiki/File:Satin_Angora.JPG

Photo by Flickr user SeeMidTN.com
www.flickr.com/photos/brent_nashville/240070817/sizes/z/in/photostream/

Photo by Flickr user Nick Bramhall
www.flickr.com/photos/black_friction/869580598/sizes/z/in/photostream/

Photo by Emma Jane Hogbin
http://commons.wikimedia.org/wiki/File%3AAngora_rabbit_post_hair_cut.jpg

Photo by Flickr user Foshie
www.flickr.com/photos/foshie/129326667/sizes/z/in/photostream

Photo Courtesy www.rabbitsorbunnies.com

Photo By by ~iROCKthouSUCK
http://irockthousuck.deviantart.com/art/Poof-134674239

References

"A Beginner's Guide to Angora Rabbit Care." Maine Angora Producers.
www.maineangoraproducers.com/begin_guide.html

"Angora (English) The British Rabbit Council.
www.thebrc.org/standards/F1-Angora.pdf

"Angora Rabbit Care Guidelines," International Association of German Angora Rabbit Breeders,
www.iagarb.com/angoracare.html

"Angora Rabbit Online Technical Manual."
AngoraRabbit.com.
https://angorarabbit.com/hutch/articles.php?cat_id=4

Bartold, Margaret. "Enteritis." National Angora Rabbit Breeders Club.
www.nationalangorarabbitbreeders.com/enteritis-article.pdf

"Breed Standard." Don's Angoras.
www.angoras.co.uk/brstand06.htm

"Breeding Angoras." C.B's French Angora Bunnies.
https://sites.google.com/site/cbsfrenchangorabunnies/breeding-angoras

"Can I have a pet rabbit?" Department of Agriculture, Fisheries and Forestry Biosecurity Queensland http://www.daff.qld.gov.au/__data/assets/pdf_file/0009/577 80/IPA-Keeping-Rabbits-As-Pets-PA15.pdf

"Feeding the Angora Rabbit & Wool Block Prevention." Avillion Farm. http://avillionfarm.com/pdflib/RabbitFeedAndWB.pdf

Glenn, Pat. "Tips for Grooming Angoras." National Angora Rabbit Breeders Club. www.nationalangorarabbitbreeders.com/tipsforgrooming.p df

"Hand-Rearing Orphan Baby Rabbits," CottonTails Rescue. www.cottontails-rescue.org.uk/handrear.asp

"Hiding Places." The Royal Society for the Prevention of Cruelty to Animals. www.rspca.org.uk/allaboutanimals/pets/rabbits/behaviour/ enrichment/hidingplaces

"History of the Angora Rabbit." Don's Angoras. http://www.angoras.co.uk/wp13/?page_id=197

"History of the Angora Rabbit." Examiner.com. www.examiner.com/article/history-of-the-angora-rabbit

Hobbs-Fothergrill, Mrs. Yvonne. "Exhibition Grooming." National Angora Rabbit Club of Great Britain. http://nationalangoraclub.webs.com/exhibition%20groomin g%20(yvonne).pdf

How to Care for Newborn Rabbits (up to 2 months old) http://www.curiousbunny.com/newborn_rabbits_detail.pdf

"How to Care for your Angora Rabbit." The Joy of Handspinning
http://joyofhandspinning.com/how-to-care-for-your-angora-rabbit/

Myxomatosis in Pet Rabbits
http://exoticpets.about.com/od/rabbitshealth/p/myxomatosis.htm

Osborn, Phill and Judy. "Keeping Angora Rabbits for Fibre." PocketFarm.co.uk. www.pocketfarm.co.uk/keeping-angora-rabbits-for-fibre/

"New Owner Guide," Appalachian Angora Rabbit Club, www.appalachianangoras.org/new-owner-guide.html

Pet Bunny Care: Grooming Your Angora Rabbit
http://voices.yahoo.com/pet-bunny-care-grooming-angora-rabbit-7044976.html?cat=53

"Rabbit – Angora Breed Profile." PetPlanet.co.uk. www.petplanet.co.uk/small_breed_profile.asp?sbid=8

"Rabbit Show Information." RabbitSingapore.org. http://rabbitsingapore.org/Rabbit%20Show%20Information%20(published).pdf

"Showing Your Rabbits." Huddersfield & District Fanciers Society. www.huddersfieldrabbits.org.uk/showingrabbits.htm

"The Time and Cost Involved in Keeping Rabbits." The Royal Society for the Prevention of Animal Cruelty. www.rspca.org.uk/imagelocator/locateasset?asset=document&assetid=1232729413756&mode=prd

Three Little Ladies Rabbitry
http://www.threelittleladiesrabbitry.com/woolblock.php

TLC for English Angoras
www.bettychuenglishangora.com/cares

.

CPSIA information can be obtained
at www.ICGtesting.com
Printed in the USA
BVOW09s2111141117

500159BV00007B/133/P